D0041672

DATE DUE

BEC 11			

GAYLORD   PRINTED IN U.S.A.

WITHDRAWN
UTSA Libraries

The Road from Thatcherism

by the same author

CRISIS IN KENYA (with K. Aaronovitch), 1947

MONOPOLY, 1955

THE RULING CLASS, 1961

ECONOMICS FOR TRADE UNIONISTS, 1964

BIG BUSINESS: CONCENTRATION AND MERGERS IN THE UK
(with M. Sawyer), 1975

THE POLITICAL ECONOMY OF BRITISH CAPITALISM
(with R. Smith, J. Gardiner, R. Moore), 1981

THE ROAD FROM THATCHERISM

The Alternative Economic Strategy

by

SAM AARONOVITCH

LAWRENCE AND WISHART
LONDON

Lawrence and Wishart Ltd
39 Museum Street
London WC1

First published, 1981
© Sam Aaronovitch, 1981

This book is sold subject to the condition that it shall not, by way of trade or otherwise, be lent, re-sold, hired out, or otherwise circulated without the publisher's prior consent in any form of binding or cover other than that in which it is published and without a similar condition including this condition being imposed on the subsequent purchaser.

Dedicated to the 'children'

Sabrina
David
Owen
Ben

Printed and bound in Great Britain at
The Camelot Press Ltd, Southampton

LIBRARY
The University of Texas
At San Antonio

Contents

Preface

As most readers will recognize, this book could not have been written without the previous work of many political and trade union activists, writers and economists. In the interest of brevity I have kept footnotes and references to a minimum and must therefore ask the forgiveness of the many unacknowledged contributors.

I have benefited from valuable comments by Mike Bleaney, Paul Levine (who also prepared the Appendix), Sheila Smith, Roger Simon and Martin Jacques. Lawrence and Wishart gave most constructive editorial help. Responsibility for what appears in the following pages is of course mine. Though short, this has not been an easy book to write, and the fact that it was finished at all owes much to the friendship, encouragement and practical support given to me by Peter Samson.

December 1980

1 Introduction

'Thatcherism' has entered popular language not simply or even mainly as an economic policy but as a vision of life which believes that the reforms and achievements, painfully fought for over decades by the democratic and labour movement in Britain, and by reformers of the most varied views, are evils which have corrupted British society and the economy with it. It therefore subjects them, and also the organizations built up with great effort and sacrifice to defend and improve the condition of the people, to the most severe attack since they were first won after the Labour victory of 1945.

It would be a mistake to think of 'Thatcherism' as the belief of a small fanatical sect which has somehow captured the leadership of the Tory Party; it represents a significant and continuous trend within that party and amongst powerful financial and industrial interests. It has become the dominant force because the main interests within the Tory Party and in big business have formed the view that only radical remedies can deal with the deep-seated problems of the economy in a way that strengthens their own class positions.

'Thatcherism' believes only radical remedies can deal with the deep-seated problems of the economy. I agree. But the radical strategy of the Tory Government represents a mixture of the very policies and doctrines which helped to bring the British economy into its present critical state. Moreover, as we shall see, the Tories are not in control of the consequences of their policies. As an industrialist remarked: 'They said a phoenix would rise from the ashes, but what if only ashes are left?'

Many people now say: we did not vote for this, and resistance grows. However, millions also feel, even when they are trying to defend themselves against attack, that the Tories are right when they say tough action is needed to resolve the problems of the economy; they do not believe that there is a credible alternative to Tory policies.

The problems of British society and the economy are deep-seated. Recognition will have to come that we cannot defend or reinstate our former economic and industrial structure: we cannot deal with the crisis by the same instruments of control and management used by previous Tory and Labour governments; we cannot advance the working people by conducting trade union struggles along traditional lines; we cannot operate in the world economy as we have done or are now trying to do; we cannot simply restore the welfare system that existed up to the mid-seventies.

If this is so, then there must be a radical alternative to the policies of the radical right. The main objective of this book is to put forward such an alternative in the most practical and credible way possible.

As a crucial part of the social and political changes needed, discussion has grown around the idea of an Alternative Economic Strategy (AES) – drawn primarily from the trade union and labour movement – an attempt, by different groups and sections who wish to challenge Toryism and the dominance of big business to formulate a *common programme*.

The argument and proposals which constitute the bulk of this book are not therefore my private invention. They arise from conferences and discussions involving many different sections of the Labour Party, the trade unions, the TUC, the Communist Party and other groups, as well as work by individual economists and theorists. But in elaborating, developing and presenting such a strategy I have had to do more than simply put together what already exists. What follows must therefore be seen as a further contribution to formulating it, a process in which I hope the readers of this book will play an active part.

The way in which the AES has evolved bears, not surprisingly, the hallmarks of the organizations which have initiated it. Some of them have been concerned with urgent and rather piecemeal proposals; or have thought of change as coming *from* government and not arising from a movement of people. The proposals have not taken properly into account the needs, experiences and perspectives of women, or of the young unemployed, or of ethnic minorities. This book cannot claim to have overcome these limitations but, with other contributions, it may stimulate thought which will develop and improve the strategy; as the movement widens and grows, new ideas and new emphases will change the way all of us think about how we want to live. With the AES, the left within the labour and trade union movement has made a bold initiative; much depends on how it is pursued and developed.

It might be useful at this point to give a brief summary of the main aims and policies of this alternative economic strategy.

Aims

To stop the waste of human and material resources which takes place through mass unemployment and under-used capacity; instead, to use and develop them to meet the needs of the people.

To increase popular involvement in all areas of life, including the control of the national economy, shifting power away from big business

To attack poverty and class inequalities as well as discrimination based on sex and colour.

Means

To expand the economy especially through large-scale public investment and current spending, including direct and indirect support for massive investment in industry.

To increase democratic control and planning over the main levers of the economy through the extension and democratization of publicly-owned industry and through planning agreements with all large enterprises, public and private.

To launch a new social strategy based on reshaping the welfare system and social services and through radical reform of the tax system.

To ensure *controlled* growth of imports so as to help domestic economic growth.

The view underlying the AES is that the future of Britain lies with its people and with the development of their skills and abilities, and that workers by hand and brain constitute the critical productive force. Tory policies, in contrast, involve the destruction of part of that force and the attempt to undermine its organizations.

The AES is not an economic system but part of a broad strategy to advance the interests of the majority of the population. The proposals in themselves do not amount to a programme for the socialist reconstruction of Britain and could gain the support of millions who do not think of themselves as socialist. However, I would hope that, in supporting these more limited proposals, such people would come to recognize the need for a more radical and socialist transformation. The policies of the AES certainly represent a challenge to the power of private capital and therefore contribute to a strategy for socialism.

It has been difficult to avoid presenting these proposals as a package; perhaps it would be better to say that it is by presenting them in this way that the reader can judge their coherence, consistency and credibility. However, these ideas are meant to be seen as a basis for action now and not as a programme waiting for a government of the left. If such action does not develop, that government will never come.

We are not playing a board game. The longer the delay in making changes, the harder they will be to make, the tougher the decisions, and the slower the improvements we could expect from them. Some of the individual proposals can of course – and no doubt will – be put into practice by Tory and right-wing Labour governments under sufficient pressure (such as certain kinds of import controls which in fact already operate to some extent). But only popular pressure and vigorous campaigning can create the conditions for a government of the left. The menacing fact that world military tension and arms spending are rising in conditions of economic crisis (as they have often done in the past) should warn us that economics and politics are inseparable.

Finally, a few words about the structure of this book.

Chapter 2 shows why the economy is in trouble. Chapter 3 explains how the 1974–9 Labour Government prepared the way for the Tory victory, and examines Tory strategy. Chapters 4–8 present the key ideas and arguments of the AES in detail. Chapter 9 deals with the political strategy involved, by way of a reply to the AES's labour movement critics – right and ultra-left – who are its determined opponents, and closes with a discussion of the situation of the Labour Party and the unions, and the kind of action which can translate the AES into everyday practice.

2 What is Wrong with the British Economy?

Obviously the problems of the British economy did not *start* with Callaghan or Thatcher, or even with Heath and Wilson – though all of them contributed, some greatly. We cannot assess the policies of the Tory Government without understanding why the British economy has got into its present state. This means taking a longer term view.

It is a crucial assumption that Britain is essentially a capitalist society, i.e. one in which the drive to accumulate profitably by the owners and controllers of capital is and has been the major force. The question for them has been: how are they to do this and deal with the obstacles in their way? But the question also arises: why is the British capitalist economy less able to expand than others, such as the West German or Japanese? We need not only an historical but a comparative view.

The dominant forces of capital and governments have sacrificed the productive base of the British economy at all crucial stages (except for world wars). This has been in striking contrast with, for instance, the policies of the ruling groups of those of our main rivals who have grown faster.

The facts of *relative* decline are not in dispute. We have grown less fast, our productivity is lower and grows more slowly; real incomes have grown more slowly; and by comparison with others we invest less and with less result. How are we to explain this?

Everyone knows that British capitalism pioneered the industrial revolution, establishing a dominant position in world manufacturing. Linked with that dominance was a trading pattern whereby the UK exchanged manufactured goods for raw materials and foodstuffs, became a lender and investor abroad on an ever-increasing scale, transported everyone's goods in her merchant ships, and provided insurance and other services on a world scale.

That world dominance could not, of course, be held for ever. In that sense, relative decline was unavoidable. The rival capitalist economies built up their domestic strength using protection and substantial state support, based on the most modern technologies. In this way they could prepare the ground for invading world markets, and challenge Britain's dominance.

The British response to this challenge was critical. Essentially it chose further imperial expansion, taking advantage of privileged markets and connections; and it expanded and exploited the financial resources and skills focused in what is conventionally called the City of London. The significance of this response was far reaching.

First, it evaded the need for large-scale modernization and reconstruction of several areas of British industry. Second, it further expanded the overseas interests and role of British-owned capital (by the beginning of the First World War, more capital was being exported than was invested at home). Third, it helped perpetuate the distance between the banks and industry; firms were mainly dependent on their own profits for expansion.

Here we have a striking contrast with West Germany and Japan. In these countries the establishment of a powerful, technologically modernized domestic base was the priority. Expansion into world markets was expected to start from that base and not as an alternative. And further, the banks and industry were closely connected, making long-term capital available at relatively low rates of interest and with longer time horizons.

This 'evasion' of the reconstruction of its domestic base has been characteristic of British capital ever since the 1880s and has been continued since 1945.

But, it will be argued, our governments have in fact made strenuous attempts to modernize the economy. Here again we find an interesting contrast with many of our major rivals. British governments have been amongst the most reluctant to intervene in the 'supply' or 'production' side of the economy. The first post-war Labour Government dismantled the war-time controls with maximum speed and pursued free trade and convertibility of currencies (not without American pressure). But as rivalry intensified, especially during the sixties, British governments were pushed into some recognition that a peace-time government-supported industrial policy was needed. The most ambitious such 'modernization' programme was that of the 1964 Labour Government; but it failed to meet the challenge.

The depth of the problem for the British economy was masked by the long wave of post-war expansion. At a number of critical points British big business and finance, together with governments, sacrificed the domestic economy to their international role and to international pressures. This was so at the time of the Korean war when the ludicrous and massive rearmament programme was launched by Hugh Gaitskell; and it was the case in 1976 when the demands of the International Monetary Fund (IMF) for deflationary measures were accepted.

The one striking moment when the Heath Government decided to ignore international constraints and initiate the expansion of the domestic economy, ended badly. It attempted this by a massive increase in credit; the outcome was only a limited rise in investment, together with a property boom and raging inflation. The methods were inappropriate and the response of capitalist and financiers was to use most of the credit available for investment in property and finance.

The broad response of big business and finance over the post-war period can be summarized under three heads:

First: *concentration and rationalization.* Independently of government but – during the 1964–70 Labour Government – with state financial help and encouragement, a large-scale merger movement took place which altered the structure of British industry and finance and concentrated economic power in fewer hands. 1979 estimates, for instance, showed that out of 1,550 industrial concerns quoted on the London Stock Exchange, the 6 largest accounted for over a quarter of the turnover and the top 180 accounted for 80%. The top 10 took 30% of pre-tax profits and owned the same proportion of net tangible assets (*Financial Times*, 30/3/79). Many thousands of firms changed ownership, and this was accompanied by a policy of rationalization which contributed to the loss of jobs from 1967 onwards.

Second: *growing interest in investment abroad and especially in Western Europe and North America.* The large firms and financial institutions (though many of them were already well-rooted abroad) set out greatly to enlarge the proportion of their overseas activities and assets. This overseas growth of British manufacturing companies is especially important. A *Labour Research* survey (January 1980) of the fifty largest UK manufacturing firms showed that one third of their output is now produced overseas; their overseas production is three times more important to them than their exports from the UK; and that overseas production has increased more rapidly than production in Britain (130% increase in the last five years compared with 117% for home production). In addition, British capital has been investing overseas at a faster rate than its main rivals.

Third: *in view of the weakening of Britain's capitalist economy within the world economy and the rising challenge from the countries of the*

Commonwealth, British governments were compelled to seek new political and economic alignments. Having first slighted the EEC, the British attempted to outflank it (with EFTA – the European Free Trade Association), and finally sought to join it. It was not possible to do this until 1972 by which time our position relative to the EEC had been further weakened and the entry terms were onerous (see also Chapter 7).

These responses clearly did little to place the British economy in a stronger and more competitive position, and this was felt even more when the world economic recession began to develop in 1973, and following the large oil-price increases.

The governments of the major capitalist countries responded to the crisis by refusing to expand their economies, even taking deflationary measures in order, they argued, to deal with the danger of inflation caused by the oil-price rise. Since the oil-price rises were deflationary (taking money out of the pockets of the main oil-importing countries), such policies deepened the crisis. From the standpoint of British governments (including the 1974 Labour Government) the hope was that West Germany, Japan, and the USA would meet the recession by policies of expansion and so permit a breathing space for the UK. However, they would not do so (as Chancellor Denis Healey frequently complained). (It needs to be said that the 1973 world recession was *not* caused by the rise in oil prices. The slow-down occurred six months *before* the price of oil was raised drastically.)

While the giant firms (especially the oil companies) and financial institutions were and are building up further international strength, the British economy continued its relative decline accentuated by the world economic crisis. The *symptoms* were to be seen in the following features:

The growth of mass unemployment especially from the sixties. From 331,000 in 1966 (a 1·4% rate) the figure of registered unemployed rose to 582,000 in 1970 (2·5%) to 1,303,000 in 1979 (5·4%) and had gone beyond 2 million (almost 9%) by December 1980.

The rising import of manufactures as a proportion of home sales. Between 1968 and 1978 the volume of manufacturing imports rose by an annual average of 5·8%; between 1975 and 1978 they had risen by 6·3% per year and in 1979 alone they rose by 15·7%.

Low levels of investment in manufacturing. Investment per head for the period 1970–4 in the UK was barely more than half that of West Germany, 45% of Japan, 44% of France, 32% of the US.

Low levels of productivity. Not surprisingly, the increase in output
per unit of investment (taking 1958–72) was almost half that of West
Germany and well below France, Japan and the US.

A substantial fall in the *rate of profit in manufacturing* in the case of
firms mainly producing within the UK – the cause and consequence
of low rates of investment and its productive use. Note, however, that
the figures for profitability normally exclude the very largest multinationals with major overseas interests.

And finally, *above-average rates of inflation.* The annual rise in
consumer prices between 1968 and 1978 for OECD countries was
7·6%, but it was 11·8% for the UK. By 1980 the gap had widened
with a UK rate of 19%, compared to 12·6% for the OECD.

De-industrialization

It is hardly surprising that the neglect of the industrial base of the
British economy has led to the now accelerating de-industrialization of
the economy. We shall discuss in the following chapter how recent
events and policies have made this worse. Here we must briefly answer
the questions: is it inevitable? And does it matter?

There is a trend in all advanced industrial countries for the *proportion*
of services and non-manufacturing activity and employment to increase. This is not in itself unconditionally good or bad: with rising
income and resources, more health, education, welfare, and personal
services (leisure, etc.) are demanded as against goods, and this can
improve the quality of life.

Moreover productivity rises faster in industry than in services, so industrial employment tends to rise less and to fall as a *proportion* of total
employment.

For Britain, however, the pace of de-industrialization raises very
serious questions. Between 1970 and 1979 employment in manufacturing fell by 17%, from 8,164,000 to 6,805,000. Given that manufacturing is crucial to employment in many regions, this absolute
fall creates *structural* unemployment. Further, it is on the manufacturing sector that much of the advances in productivity depend, and it is
the export of manufactured goods which has been the major earner of
foreign exchange. Even as late as 1977 manufacturing exports provided
42% of foreign exchange compared with 18% earned by services,
shipping and civil aviation. That surplus of manufactured exports over
manufactured imports has been drastically cut. Exports from services

cannot possibly replace the foreign exchange earnings needed, nor can they provide alternative jobs where they are needed if the industrial run-down continues on its present scale.

However, those who believe that de-industrialization is a good thing argue that in place of creating new assets within the UK which earn lower rates of return, 'we' (British capitalists and financiers) should be enabled to acquire assets overseas where rates of return are higher and which would lead to interest and dividend payments flowing back into the UK. But when North Sea oil ceases to meet all our needs, we shall be an economy mainly dependent on foreign earnings. And these earnings would go whenever their owners decided to shift their headquarters or personal residences abroad. Why should they stay here anyway, if the bulk of their income is overseas and they can take advantage of lower taxes through tax havens, and other measures?

The de-industrialization debate only underlines the point that the main thrust of government and big business policy has been to try to reconcile a limited modernization and reorganization of the UK economy with a strengthening of the world role of British capital. The result is a half-hearted and contradictory modernization programme as shown in the experience of the 1964–79 Labour Government. How can profits from UK manufacturing show great improvement if there is little investment? And how could capitalists decide to invest on a large scale in the UK if there is little prospect of economic growth within that economy? Between 1968 and 1978 industrial output in the UK grew at less than half the rate of OECD countries.

The economic crisis, as typically the case in capitalist economies, is seen as a time of shake-out, when 'surplus' capital can be written down in value, manpower got rid of, and the weaker capitalists go to the wall. Governments have seen economic crisis as a moment when they can legitimize and justify their rationalizations, cutting back planned public spending and allowing unemployment to rise.

Moreover, the slowing of world economic growth and trade has also been accompanied by a rise in international tension and by a renewed arms race. There is now a global stockpile of 60,000 nuclear weapons and a new wave of preparation of chemical weapons is under way. British military spending, already high in international terms, has begun to rise once again in absolute terms and as a proportion of national income. In 1980, estimated UK spending on defence was over £11,000 million; the Government plans to increase this by 3% each year. The effects of rising military tension have combined with the growing difficulties of the UK economy further to expand developments of the internal security forces, both military and police. The key issue for these forces is dealing with civil disorders, including strikes.

With this in mind, we must now take the argument about post-war British capitalism a stage further. One of the most prominent features of the Labour and Tory governments since 1970 has been the extent to which they have convinced themselves that they cannot combine even limited modernization with Britain's world role, unless they weaken decisively the bargaining capacity of the trade union and labour movement. The concern of dominant business and political circles may be presented as two-fold.

At the political level, even though the Labour Party in post-war Britain has lost the peak share of votes it held in 1945, the electoral system continues to make it possible for it to form governments. The Tory Party has faced the prospect of losing its 'natural' position as a party of the nation. The danger it sees is that within the Labour Party the left, however limited, is a force to be reckoned with and has the capacity to grow. One measure of the Tory and big business fear was the ferocity with which they attacked Tony Benn as Minister of Industry and secured his removal to a less 'sensitive' area (Energy).

This fear was accentuated over the post-war period because at different times the base of the Labour Party in the trade unions appeared 'vulnerable' to a left advance with, for instance, changes in the leadership of the engineering and transport workers unions, as well as others.

At the industrial level, the post-war period has seen an uninterrupted growth of the trade unions and of affiliation to the TUC, now nearly 12·2 million. Trade union organization has grown amongst white-collar workers and amongst women; it has become very strong in the public sector and, despite the slow growth or even decline in the number of manual workers, even there there has been an increase in the proportion organized in trade unions.

For a large part of the post-war period the existence of almost full employment and indeed of labour shortages made it easier for the unions to bargain, and in that atmosphere a powerful shop-floor and shop stewards' organization was built up. That strength, once established, has proved hard for business to dislodge.

Unlike such countries as West Germany, France, and Japan, British capitalism did not have a labour surplus in the countryside or geographically near it on which to draw. The trade union movement therefore was in a better position to challenge attempts to cut real wages and worsen conditions of work.* It was clearly capable of acting as a powerful obstructive force to big business and right-wing strategies. For these reasons, the trade unions became the focus of sustained ideological attack in which the mass media played (and plays) a major role, arguing essentially that the unions obstructed necessary modern-✓ ization and rationalization programmes, were responsible for inflation because of their pressure for increased money wages, and were beyond the law and had become a state within the state.

In fact, the trade unions had pursued essentially defensive or reactive policies, concentrating on their sectional battles; the TUC had only a limited coordinating role. Its power was real but it worked (when used) only in limited directions (such as for wage increases and against anti-trade union legislation).

Paradoxical as it may seem, it was precisely this defensiveness and limited view of its national role which helped the anti-trade union campaign and contributed to the political isolation of the trade union movement, with consequences which we examine in the next chapter.

But big business and right-wing political circles (including those within the Labour Party) came increasingly to believe that they could not sustain even their limited modernization and world roles without removing this major obstruction. The fact that the Labour Government had to abandon *In Place of Strife* in 1969, that the miners defeated a key aspect of Edward Heath's strategy in 1973–4, that the public-sector workers broke through government wage restraint policies in 1977 – these events and others created a mood amounting to an obsession that the impasse created by the strength of the trade union and shop steward movement had to be broken.

Against the background of economic decline, the Tory Government has thus mounted the most sustained and radical attempt we have so far experienced to break this impasse and impose a new set of rules. But we still need to look in more detail at how it was able to become such a force and what are its consequences.

* The *real* wage is the 'basket' of goods and services workers can buy with the money they receive as wages. If, for instance, wages rise but the prices of goods and services rise faster, then the *real* wage falls.

3 From 'Labourism' to 'Thatcherism': Why Did It Happen?

The Tory victory of May 1979 was a sharp blow to millions of Labour supporters and to the Labour Party itself, but it was prepared for by the 1974–9 Labour Government. We should not underestimate the scale of Labour's defeat and we need also to see it as part of a longer run decline. At its post-war peak Labour polled nearly 50% of the vote and about 40% of those eligible to vote. With the exception of 1966 both shares fell steadily. In 1979 Labour polled 37% of the vote — its lowest post-war figure, and 29% of the electorate. By 1980 individual membership of the Labour Party had 'officially' also fallen by about one-third from its 1950 peak of 900,000, but was probably well below 600,000.

Nor should we understate the Tory victory. The Tory Party has also faced a fall in its share of the vote and of the electorate from its peak of nearly 50% of the vote in 1955. But in 1979, bearing in mind the increase in the Liberal challenge, from 110 to 576 candidates, and that the 1955 figures included the Ulster Unionist, the Tory share may not have fallen very substantially below its peak figure.

In some areas in 1979 the Tories made significant inroads into the working-class vote, including that of trade unionists and their families. Their gains were substantially less in Scotland and the North, although, contrary to numerous statements, there was a swing — though very small — to the Tories in Scotland.

Of course the Tory victory did not represent a majority mandate: both Labour and Tory parties have benefited from our undemocratic electoral system. The decline in the two-party system through the rise of Liberal and Nationalist parties, together with a decline in the number of those voting, has meant that parties with only a minority of the votes cast, and an even smaller proportion of the electorate as a whole, can win parliamentary majorities. In May 1979 the Tory Party polled 45% of the vote but only 34% of the electorate. It is in that sense that we can perceive the fragility of the mandate claimed by the Tories.

What, some may say, does the size of the Tory victory or of the

Labour defeat in 1979 matter now, as opposition grows daily to the Tory policies? If the causes for Labour's defeat and the victory of the Tories are not understood, we are in fact depending upon the 'swing of the pendulum' for a Labour victory: the same, or worse, mistakes will be repeated and must in due course lead to even greater disillusion.

The lessons of the 1974–9 Labour Government

In very broad terms the main criticism to be made of the 1974–9 Labour Government is that it accepted the logic of Britain's dominant capitalist groups: the attempt to combine a limited modernizing and rationalizing programme with an expansion of their world role without any major changes in class and social relationships. That meant that the costs of adjustment had to be carried by the working class. The Government's problems were made worse by the world recession which developed from 1973. As a result, at critical moments, Labour sacrificed the interests of the domestic economy to its international role.

To say this is not to argue, as some do, that the Labour Party is no different from the Tory Party. The Labour Party remains predominantly a party of the organized workers and their families; its main base is the trade union movement; and it has been the centre for powerful currents of reform in all branches of welfare. Because of this the Labour Government, subjected to that pressure, had to repeal the Tory Industrial Relations Act, allowed the formation and rise of the British National Oil Corporation (BNOC), introduced some form of price and dividend control, and instituted many valuable reforms in the Health and other welfare services. It also put through parliament the 1975 Sex Discrimination Act and Employment Protection Act and the 1976 Race Relations Act. In fact, had these things not been done, the Labour Government would have found it impossible to gain support for what proved to be very damaging policies.

What then are the charges to be made against the 1974–9 Labour Government? There are five which I consider the most important.

First, as shown by the rapid increase in unemployment from 1973, it abandoned what had been an accepted post-war consensus – the maintenance of full employment. It turned its back on the idea, based on Keynesian arguments, that governments should and could pursue high levels of employment through fiscal and monetary policies which maintained high levels of demand. James Callaghan put it concisely when he argued that he no longer believed that you could spend your way out of a recession – precisely what Keynes did believe. Inflation was seen as the main enemy and the government moved increasingly to monetarist arguments as its justification for deflation. Pressure from the IMF was certainly a powerful contributory factor, but it corresponded to views already held within the Government, the Treasury and the Bank of England.

Second, in the name of fighting inflation, it sought to reduce real incomes, but – remembering Edward Heath's experience – to do so on the basis of trade union agreement. This was the substance of the Social Contract endorsed by the TUC in 1975. In return for wage restraint (which, with rising prices, meant a fall in real incomes) the Government undertook to pursue policies to reduce unemployment, increase government spending on social services (especially on housing, child benefit schemes, pensions and health) and to take powers to control prices and dividends.

While making some concessions, the main thrust of Labour Government policy was to cut real wages and redistribute resources from labour to capital. It made it increasingly clear that it rejected the 1973 Labour Party conference programme. Inequality was not reduced during its term of office but probably increased.

Third, it severely cut planned public expenditure and began the process of reducing it as a proportion of gross domestic product (GDP): from a peak of 27% spent in 1975/6 on goods and services GDP fell to a planned 23% for 1979/80. As it happens, the Labour Government's cuts fell mainly on capital spending rather than current spending plans, so the impact was less visible to the consumer; but when the Tory Government's cuts in planned spending came later, capital spending had already been severely axed and more weight had to fall on current spending. Hence the rising opposition even of some Tory councils to recent cuts.

Fourth, it continued the policy of entry into the EEC, and the renegotiated terms left Britain with a growing burden, while its ability to pay was reduced. Joining the EEC when a world recession was beginning further limited government policy options.

In 1975 the Labour Government in a referendum secured a majority vote for remaining within the EEC; it was widely agreed that the result was a defeat for the left. What was not so widely understood was that it was a defeat for the people. The opinion polls in 1979 and 1980 began to show some recognition of that.

Fifth, it watered down into very thin gruel the bold proposals of the 1973 Labour Party conference which called for 'a fundamental and irreversible shift in the balance of power and wealth in favour of working people and their families'. The proposed National Investment

Board was in practice made into a minor merchant bank, apart from its holdings in the nearly bankrupted British Leyland and Rolls-Royce. The proposed planning agreements by which the giant private and public enterprises were to be brought within an overall policy of expansion became purely voluntary and only two token ones were ever signed – with Chrysler (a condition of government aid) and with the National Coal Board. The weight of industrial policy was placed on the National Economic Development Council (NEDC) and the Sector Working Parties which had no secure national framework and no independent powers. And so the story could go on.

Admittedly this indictment oversimplifies the record of the Labour Government, but it provides the key to what happened. I am not arguing that the 1973 Labour Party conference proposals, which could have been the basis for a radical government programme for the 1974 session, would have been received by the British electorate with open arms. I *am* arguing that the policies actually adopted prepared the ground for Labour's defeat.

How the ground for Thatcherism was prepared

The Tory Party went into the 1979 elections in buoyant and aggressive spirit; the Labour Party enterd it defensively, asking to be judged on its record. The contrast with 1945 could hardly be more striking. What were the Tories able to take hold of and exploit?

First and obviously, they could use the disillusion that had grown up within the labour and trade union movement and amongst Labour supporters as a result of the attack on real wages, their experience of the Social Contract, and the growing threat to jobs. The revolt of the public sector workers (the 'winter of discontent'), and the trade union rejection of the Government's 5% wage limit, contributed to that disillusion at the same time as it became valuable material for the anti-Labour, anti-trade union campaign.

Second, Labour had become identified as the party of state intervention and state ownership as remedies for Britain's problems. However, the direction, policies and structure of the nationalized industries, and those acquired by default, like British Leyland, were bureaucratic and even despotic, and decision-making was far removed from those who worked in them or who used them as consumers. In addition, the pressure to make them conform to commercial criteria, as in public transport, contributed to policies which alienated workers and consumers alike. Nationalization and public ownership therefore became dirty words.

Third, in spite of many innovations and improvements in different areas, the pressure on the public services led overall to deteriorating standards while the need for them grew. At the same time millions of people were drawn into the tax net as a result of inflation, and were told that they were paying for services which they did not always feel were satisfactory, or which were given to people who did not pay tax ('scroungers', 'students', etc., a view which the popular press fostered). This weakened popular support for financing services based on high levels of personal taxation (note that for the lower-paid workers the *marginal* tax rate was very high indeed).

It is easy to see that this helped the Tory campaign for promised tax cuts, reductions in public spending, and for a tougher line towards those who 'scrounged' on the state.

Fourth, the Labour Government had waged a powerful campaign identifying trade union pressure for wage increases as the main cause of inflation and therefore as the main source of Britain's economic problems. This theme was happily supported by the Tory Party, business circles and the mass media, and had as its object the political isolation of the trade union and shop steward movement. As I have suggested earlier, the trade union movement did not respond to this with a popular counter-campaign designed to win allies for a different strategy, but acted — as it has done traditionally — defensively and on a sectional basis. These weaknesses were helpful to the Tory campaign. The left could also be represented (and often presented itself) as simply wanting more of the same increasingly unpopular policies of state intervention and public ownership.

Finally there was the spreading mood of frustration, tension and anger which drew on a number of different sources: the sense of national decline, the threat of social breakdown in the inner-city areas, and growing feelings of insecurity. The Labour/Tory consensus, which had ruled through most of the fifties and sixties, was breaking down during the seventies, releasing ugly feelings and ideas. This was the basis for the growth in racialism, exploited by the Tories, and their use of the theme of law and order with the demand for tough action to deal with 'scroungers' and muggers.

The Tory campaign was unscrupulous, ferocious and well orchestrated.* This is why it is dangerous to underestimate the

---

* British companies gave the Tory Party and supporting organizations a record £2·55 million – the insurance companies being specially generous; none gave money to the Labour Party; of the £1,500 received by the Liberal Party from companies, £1,000 came from the Playboy Club!

significance of the Tory victory even in an atmosphere of growing resistance to Tory actions.

Moreover, because of changes which had taken place within the Tory Party and amongst sections of business on which it rested so heavily, the Tories had the ability to exploit this situation with much ruthlessness, and to pose against the caricature of 'socialism' a completely different image.

As with so many other difficult questions, it is only too easy to over-simplify complicated political processes, but I want to consider two crucial features of this phenomenon.

First, the defeat of Heath's strategy at the hands of the miners and others contributed to the feeling, which had already begun to inspire the Tories in the 1970 elections, that the old era of consensus politics (Butskellism as it came to be called because of the policies of the Tory Rab Butler and Labour leader Hugh Gaitskell) could not deal with the problems facing British capitalism as it entered the seventies, nor rescue the Tory Party from the danger of decline. Far more radical right policies were needed to break the impasse. This brought to the forefront those elements within the Tory Party who advocated such radical changes.

A second component was the growing irritation of sections of employers (notably the Engineering Employers' Federation) with the strong bargaining power of the unions, especially on the shop floor; they fought within the Confederation of British Industry (CBI), as well as publicly, for more drastic policies. The emphasis was at all times on cutting public spending, diminishing the nationalized sector, and curbing the power of the unions. Their desire to 'free' the labour market became obsessive.

To combine these elements effectively and to acquire a popular basis needed a single-minded political thrust based on a clear-cut set of ideas which could confront and challenge the Labour party. Suitable ideologies such as monetarism* were to hand which could take effective advantage of the ground already prepared. The Tory argument ran along the following lines.

Inflation is the enemy to be defeated; and according to monetarist doctrine inflation arises because the supply of money has expanded

* In a technical sense, monetarism can be defined as the belief that increases in the general price level are caused by a prior rise in the money supply; but underlying this view and associated with it is a theory of the economy based on the perfection of the 'market'.

at a greater rate than the supply of goods. Prices can be brought down if the supply of money is restricted. The major single source of increased money supply is government spending more than it raises in taxation (that difference is the Public Sector Borrowing Requirement [PSBR]). The most important contribution to reducing inflation is therefore the reduction in the PSBR, which is the only real way in which government can influence what happens in the economy.

Not only is increased government spending (which has increased the PSBR) the most powerful source of inflation, but it means that government takes money out of the pockets of those who earn it and decides how it shall be spent. Individuals should be free to decide for themselves how they spend their money, preferring if they wish private education or health to public provision. In addition, the Tories argue, state spending has created a vast and expensive bureaucracy. The expansion of the public welfare services has also encouraged many people to prefer the dole and social security to honest work; perhaps the greater part of our unemployment (it is suggested) is voluntary. Britain needs, in contrast, a revival of the spirit of self-help and entrepreneurship. We should return – say the Tories – to the old idea that the 'market' knows best. It allocates resources according to the wishes of those with money to spend, it rewards the efficient and bankrupts, rightly, the inefficient.

For those who fail to respond to this harsh doctrine, the Tories promised harsh punishment and, for the 'deviant' young, 'short sharp shocks'. They had a special word also about immigrants and ethnic minorities; the Conservative Election Manifesto of 1979 spoke of 'persistent fears about levels of immigration' and called for firm immigration control.

It is obvious that, taken together, these ideas represented a total rejection not only of the socialist but also of the reform and democratic tradition which has been a powerful strand in Britain's history and has achieved significant advances.

A summary guide to Tory practice

The Tory Government has carried through a large-scale deflation of the economy using high interest rates (flowing from its monetary policy), the high exchange rate, cuts in public spending, cash limits on nationalized industries (obliging them to sack workers and close plants as well as push up their prices), and severe increases in indirect taxation.

These measures combined have cut back demand not only for the goods and services of the public sector but *even more* of the private sector; they have led to massive increases in unemployment and short-time working.

In terms of Tory strategy, therefore, the Government has created what it believed to be the necessary conditions for weakening the bargaining power of the trade unions, reducing the pressure for increased wages, and compelling firms to rationalize or to go to the wall.

The process has begun of reducing the size of the nationalized sector: by plant closures (in steel); selling off assets (BP and some holdings of the National Enterprise Board), with further plans to hive off profitable sections or bring in private capital (into British Airways for instance).

The dismantling of welfare services has been started and favourable conditions created for the increase in private medical schemes and private education. Control over local authority spending has been tightened; the Local Authority Act drastically reduces such financial autonomy as local authorities have had.

The high interest rates together with the high rate of exchange (both important elements of government policy) have put severe pressure on the cash resources of firms, made imports much cheaper, and exports much less competitive.

The Government has abolished all that remained of exchange controls and made foreign investment easier. This has given fresh encouragement to a process already under way. There has been a striking increase in British investment in the EEC and in North America; giant firms and banks have recently made large-scale acquisitions in the USA; and – since the ending of exchange controls – British financial institutions, such as pension funds, insurance companies and unit trusts, have invested more money in the shares of overseas companies than in the ordinary shares of British companies (*Financial Times*, 24/10/80). That outflow will increase when British interest rates become less attractive compared with other countries.

The Tory Employment Act has removed protection from unfair dismissal for hundreds of thousands of people, weakened the possibilities of solidarity action, including the power to picket in support, attacked the employment conditions of working women, and opened the way for more restrictive codes of practice such as those already issued on picketing.

The Government has bluntly said that it gives military spending and the strengthening of law and order great priority and has acted accordingly. Moreover, the attacks on well-established democratic and social reforms have become so many and so frequent that it is difficult even for close observers of government behaviour to monitor the range of the onslaught. The damage now being done will be hard to reverse in areas of planning and development, education, health, and welfare.

Contradictions in policy

This summary guide does not constitute an *assessment* of Tory strategy; to do that we must examine certain parts of its policy more closely. The Tory leadership has tried to form a view of the overall interests of British capitalism and its survival – especially of the dominant groups of finance, trade and industry. The exact policies it pursues obviously depend on its vision of how the economy works and what its mechanisms are. If it misunderstands these mechanisms its policies will give perverse and unintended results, even though they may also give some of the things it wants. Further, if the Tories cannot defeat the resistance which they know they are bound to face then they must confront electoral defeat, or abandon democratic procedures altogether.

If this is true, then the *precise* ideology adopted by the Tory leadership becomes important. If it gets its view of society wrong, it will fail to protect either the short- or long-term interests of British capital. (Even so, the Tory Government may survive if those who oppose it get their vision even more wrong!)

Tory policies and objectives are being implemented in a world not under their control and with mechanisms which do not work as they think. To take three aspects: deflation in conditions of economic crisis; the control of the money supply; and the rate of inflation.

First, *deflation*. The Government, as we have shown, has pursued a severe deflationary policy deliberately designed to create a great deal of slack in the economy, especially of labour. But this has been carried through in conditions of a cyclical downturn, not only of the British, but of the major capitalist economies. So the Tories have cut demand severely when it was already falling; the scale of the depression has been greater than they expected, and they have been unwilling to believe the forecasts made by the Government's own economic models.

In addition, further factors have come into play. The high interest rate which the Government has insisted on as vital to choke off the rising tide of credit has brought with it a flood of money from abroad. This in turn has helped to keep the exchange rate of the pound riding high, reinforcing the support already given by North Sea oil. The result is to give a bonus to importers and a penalty to exporters in conditions in which competition for markets is becoming more acute. The pressure on manufacturing has intensified to a degree which probably goes well beyond the initial calculations of Tory ministers and puts them under a barrage of criticism from their supporters. Registered unemployment in the second half of 1980 was rising by 100,000 a month; the press daily reports closures, redundancies and bankruptcies. Industrial output at the moment of writing (October 1980) showed a further absolute fall.

Slices of British manufacturing industry are being eliminated; those in danger include vehicles, carpets, artificial fibres, footwear, scientific instruments, clothing, glass, paper and board; and this does not exhaust the list, quite apart from the destruction of a substantial part of our steel making capacity. In turn this has had an impact on new investment in manufacturing which in 1980 will, it is estimated, fall by 10% over 1979 with a further fall of 15% in prospect for 1981. Even worse, UK investment in comparison with other EEC countries (including Ireland) is at the bottom of the league, so that our main European rivals are improving their capacity and productive power relative to the UK. This means that taken together with the already severe import penetration, even with a revival in the economy, imports will tend to gain ground; the process of de-industrialization will grind remorselessly on.

In these crisis conditions the large multinationals especially are carrying through a rigorous policy of rationalization, shutting down less profitable plants, shifting operations to other centres (outside as well as within the UK). *They* of course expect to be stronger and to survive the blast, at the expense of a substantial part of the profit base of British industry.

An expanding and regenerated British industry on a more efficient basis is therefore an unlikely outcome. But the dominant Tory vision makes the Tories *less* able to respond to these difficulties precisely because they are trying to use remedies which have little application to the problems of British capitalism in the eighties.

Second, *the Tory strategy for controlling the money supply and reducing the PSBR both in absolute terms and as a proportion of GDP.* The familiar theoretical argument is that inflation is uniquely the result of expansion in the money supply (other things being equal). Therefore if you reduce the money supply by 10%, prices, after a lag, will fall by 10%. Since government, by borrowing from the banks more than it gets in taxes, expands the money supply, cutting the PSBR is a vital part of cutting the money supply. We should add that reducing the money supply involves high interest rates which also have the effect of attracting funds from abroad and making the exchange rate higher than it would otherwise be. This higher exchange rate makes imports cheaper. According to monetarist theory the link between high interest rates and the price level comes about because goods internationally traded can do so only at one price; as a result British manufacturers will have to meet the lower prices; they will therefore cut labour costs and keep down wage increases. In turn, as this spreads through the economy, inflation will fall.

In so far as the Government can be said to be acting on the basis of this view (and this is certainly true of Margaret Thatcher, Nigel Lawson, and Keith Joseph, for instance), it has clearly blundered. Inflation is not caused by changes in the money supply but is the outcome of a number of struggles for resources involving government, monopolistic firms and class interests. Furthermore, although the money supply does play a part in the inflationary process, it is hard to define, even harder actually to measure, and much harder still to control (even assuming, which one would not be entitled to, that what is measurable is what one needs to control). Companies have been forced to borrow from the banks even at high rates of interest to avoid bankruptcy and this has increased the chosen measure of money supply. In addition, other government measures such as the abolition of exchange controls have brought into being ingenious new methods of financing which sidestep and invalidate government controls.

Devastating criticism on this score has come from the most varied circles as the measure of money supply chosen by the Government has been rising by about 15% as compared with the target of 7–11%.

If the Government's theory were correct, nothing can prevent the rate of inflation being well over 15% in about two years (which is the time-lag thought to operate). Needless to say, it will not accept this conclusion from its own theory!

Reducing the PSBR is of course a vital part of the strategy for reducing the money supply. But here again, the PSBR has proved difficult to control. The most obvious reason is that, as government policy combined with depression drags the economy down, the numbers receiving unemployment pay rise, and more people go on to social security; in other words, the scale of government spending rises faster than the cuts it is able to make. In addition, the cuts have met with growing resistance from local authorities; the cash limits on nationalized industries have had to be modified under pressure; and defence costs have soared. The Government's response, with recession ✓ forcing up the PSBR, has been to make even more drastic cuts, putting more people on the dole and social security in order to finance the costs of its deflationary policies.*

Many people, incidentally, forget that government borrowing at very high rates of interest creates a large burden of debt to be met in the future on a scale that would be intolerable if the rate of inflation were to be brought down substantially. The high rates offered by the Government have made many observers believe that it has no confidence that it will succeed. The instrument that has worked most effectively is the high exchange rate – by severely damaging Britain's manufacturing industries!

This brings me directly to the third aspect – *the control of the rate of inflation*. What the Government managed to do in its first fifteen months' existence was to organize a rapid increase in the inflation rate. From mid-1979 to mid-1980 it added $8\frac{1}{2}$% to price increases by way of: increased VAT, adding $3\frac{3}{4}$% to the retail price index; higher local authority rates following reduced government grants, adding 1%; reduced support to nationalized industries, adding $\frac{3}{4}$%; higher national insurance contributions, adding $\frac{1}{2}$%; the agreement to raise food prices through CAP $\frac{3}{4}$%, and the increase in interest rates, adding a further $1\frac{3}{4}$%. The outcome has been *deflation* and *inflation* at the same time.

The conflicts are of course not just between the theory and the reality. There is the conflict between different interests. To some extent the theory is used as a justification. Monetarism, for instance, has the merit of appearing as a *technical* solution (i.e. solve the problems of inflation by reducing the money supply), independent of capitalist class interests around the common objective of reducing the rate of inflation.

What is supposed to happen is that, as monetary pressure cuts demand, this leads to a fall in price (or reduction in the rate of increase). But, though prices do come under pressure, all past experience shows that the *main* effect is not to cut prices but to cut output and jobs, which is the opposite of what the monetarists believe. If anything, in all but the very short term, falling demand means costs must be spread over a

* For every 1% drop in economic growth, the PSBR rises by £1 billion. For each 1% increase in growth, the PSBR is reduced by £1 billion (*Bank of England Quarterly Bulletin*, September 1980).

smaller output; so unit costs rise, and firms try to raise prices accordingly. If they cannot, they go out of business.

Another consequence which the Tory Government expected is that, with the depression, the ability of workers to bargain for higher money wages would diminish, wage costs would therefore fall, and prices could be cut or investment made more profitable, with good effects on productivity. In conditions where inflation is still rising this is obviously a call for a cut in real incomes.

Not surprisingly this policy has met determined resistance both in the private and public sector. Despite efforts to show that the size of pay settlements in the private sector was falling, average settlements in the annual wage round up to 31 July 1980 were around 18–20%, slightly *higher* than in the nationalized industries, and *considerably higher* than in the so-called 'tax-dependent' public services (once account is taken of the staged increases arising from the Comparability Commission headed by Professor Clegg).

Some groups of workers have certainly been pushed against the wall (amongst vehicle workers, British Leyland, Talbot and Vauxhall). The ground for fierce battles in the future for comparability is being prepared.

In any case it is becoming clear to many people that accepting lower rates of money wages will not preserve their jobs, a point which has come out clearly in the textile and steel industries. There is little trade-off there between less money and job security. What determines job prospects is the level of demand and the scale of investment. But here the Government offers not bread but stones.

It is true that higher productivity would reduce the cost for each unit of output and this could help to keep prices down. But though the Government says it wants increased productivity, its policies produce the opposite. There is a great deal of evidence to show that productivity rises when output is growing and falls when output is falling; and in addition, as pointed out earlier, the fall in productivity *increases* the cost for each unit produced and so tends to push up prices.

Tory strategy clearly has run into difficulties, some of which result from a mistaken view of the way the system works. But of course the Tories are acting completely in their class interests when they try to shift the balance of bargaining power towards business and away from the working people. If they could do this quickly, the way would be open for them to change some of their policies and make use of increased state intervention, changing their leaders and theories if necessary. From all that has been said it is clear that the greatest victims of Tory strategy are the poorest and the least-organized: the children, the young, the school-leavers, the old, the sick, the unemployed, one-parent families, and part-time workers. The burden of Tory policy falls on increasing numbers of wage and salaried workers as insecurity rises and real standards are attacked. It falls on those professionally concerned with the social services as they try to cope with morale-destroying cuts. It falls on whole communities as they are left without industries and jobs; it also aggravates the position of the already deprived in the inner-city areas, and puts increasing pressure on women as mothers, as lower-paid workers and as housewives coping with falling family incomes.

The Tory Government expects those who are politically hostile to it to resist. But its leadership faces another threat: the erosion of its own electoral support and criticisms of many of its policies from its main power-base in business and finance.

There is a great deal of evidence to show that growing numbers of businessmen have become uneasy over the fact that it is firms in the manufacturing sector which have been hit exceptionally hard by Tory policies. The protests have focused on high interest rates and the high exchange rate. Starting with the regional committees of the Confederation of British Industry in areas such as Wales and West Midlands, the CBI nationally has been obliged to argue for specific changes in policy; its call, however, has been for much tougher government action in cutting public spending, alongside reducing the rate of interest. But this does not resolve the difficulties, because there are industries – like the construction industry – largely dependent on government spending.

In the depression to which government policy has contributed much damage has also been done to small- and middle-sized businesses. During 1980 company liquidations were running at twice the rate of 1979 (in October 1980 at about 130 a week).

It is difficult to measure the political impact of government policy on its own supporters but the increasingly critical tone coming from economic commentators in newspapers like the *Financial Times* and *The Times* reflects widespread concern.

The basis for wide-ranging opposition to the policies of the Government is clearly becoming stronger. Pressure within the power-base of the Tory Party will grow, even more powerfully if it believes its electoral prospects are in danger. None of this, however, means that the Tory defeat is inevitable.

There are important reasons why such a defeat should not be taken for granted. Many Tory supporters and sections of capital believe they must accept the fact that individual firms and groups will be hurt in the interests of the class as a whole if capitalism is to survive. But in addition, amongst those affected badly by Tory policies, there are sources of division as pressure mounts. Many still believe in the Tories' arguments. There are divisions between those who have enough 'clout' or other bargaining advantages and can keep up with inflation, and those who cannot and who feel resentful (an important source of anti-trade union feeling). There are differences to be played upon between workers in the public service sector and those in private industry. There are sources of division between the large numbers of long-term unemployed and young school-leavers, and those in jobs. Finally, there are potential conflicts between people who benefit from cheap imports and those working in industries being threatened by the same imports, remembering that families contain consumers as well as workers.*

The Tory Government will certainly do everything it can to exploit these differences and use them, perhaps, in a further turn to the right. There are, after all, *more* reactionary 'solutions' that can be attempted. In any case, some room for manoeuvre can come from an actual shift in Tory policies (even including a change in leadership), and use can still be made of the mounting revenues from North Sea oil to offset tax cuts or higher public spending, especially as election time approaches.

It would be wrong to rely on the defeat of the Tory Government by some spontaneous growth of discontent; and equally wrong to believe that the anti-Tory movement can be based on a return to things as they were. The organized labour movement, without doubt, is the crucial and central force which can challenge the Tory Government; but if the aim is not only to defeat it but to bring about a major change in direction, the movement must exercise a very high order of political leadership. It must be able to unite all the forces amongst the working people; it has to help create an association of many different groups and movements around a common programme inspired by a different vision of what life should be like.

This cannot be done without an overall strategy, to the economic aspects of which the rest of this book is devoted.

* The Tory Party may also benefit from changes in constituency boundaries now in prospect.

4 Expansion: Why and How?

In 1980 British industry began to sink rapidly as the crisis in Britain deepened. Apart from the United States all our main capitalist rivals experienced a growth in industrial output in 1980, estimates ranging from 1% in France to 8% in Japan; in contrast British industrial output fell more than 9%. This is no longer just relative decline but *an absolute fall*. The prospects for 1981 and beyond are grim in terms of economic growth, employment and trade. Yet the Tory Government, we have seen, believes – or rather says – that deflation will cure British industry. Margaret Thatcher, at the very moment unemployment rose above two million, maintained the correctness of government policy; she was 'undaunted'.

Understandably the immediate focus is on immediate proposals for action, but in terms of broad economic policy the debate over several years has centred on the need to raise the rate of the growth of the economy over a long period, especially to deal with rising unemployment. Any alternative economic strategy must therefore deal with this central question of economic expansion.

Some argue that economic growth can alone deal with the problems of Britain and meet the expectations of the people. 'We need a bigger cake' is a familiar theme; but it is an argument often used to sidestep the question as to how our existing resources are used and distributed. There is not only the matter of wasteful expenditure (like much military spending), or the burden of taxation on different classes, but also the emphasis to be given to health, education and welfare services. So others argue that there is no need to make all change dependent on growth, which in the past has damaged the environment, rapidly using up non-renewable resources, and worsened the quality of life.

Why?

The argument for economic growth has therefore to be made. Why should we want the output of goods and services to grow at a faster rate in Britain than in the past?

Because there is much unsatisfied need for both goods and services and because new needs are always arising, especially if more and more people are given the chance to develop their abilities. Moreover, faster growth creates a better climate for innovation and development. Greater productivity in producing goods means more resources available for services and for leisure. Growth in output of goods other countries want can provide the foreign currency for the goods and services we both need and wish to import from abroad. And if we are to contribute to the economic welfare of the less-developed countries, we require the extra resources arising from faster growth.

Must more rapid industrial growth mean eating up non-renewable resources like oil at record rates? Not if effort is put into energy conservation and into new renewable forms of energy. Whether it must also mean more pollution is a matter of social policy and the use of investment to prevent it.

But 'faster growth' is a vague phrase. *What* rate of growth? There are good reasons for thinking that Japanese rates of growth (whether the 8% of 1980 or the 16% of previous years) are to be avoided. They involve disregard of all environmental and welfare considerations (unrestrained urban growth, massive pollution, rapid changes in life styles, etc.), aggressive and disruptive behaviour on world markets, and other undesirable effects.

In the past the TUC and other bodies have looked at various target rates of growth, and for a long time the benefits and possibility of the British economy growing at 6% per year was frequently put forward. However, between 1967–77 industrial output in the UK rose by 1·5% per year (1·1% excluding oil and gas). It seems unlikely that a 6% rate of growth could be reached and sustained over a long period. A government determined to expand the economy out of a depression would get quite high rates of growth but, apart from that 'lift', we would surely be happy with a steady 3% to 4% rate of growth in output for some time to come. Even this remains speculative, without a detailed model of the economy, but it is not too far removed from the ideas of expansion-minded economists who have made use of such models.

The point must be emphasized: it is not a matter of growth for its own sake; the direction and distribution of its yield are inseparable. We want full employment, but not the kind we can get from a war economy. We want increased productivity, but not to throw hundreds of thousands into a waste land and leave growing numbers of youngsters with no hope of working.

What policies can expand the economy and in what directions?

Much of the debate has taken the form of an argument as to whether 'Keynesianism' has failed in the past and whether 'Keynesian' measures can work in the future.

The idea that governments should be forced to commit themselves to policies of full employment is not, as sometimes suggested, a 'Keynesian' notion, but a long-standing position taken by the labour and socialist movements. Keynes saw what Marxists and radical economists had long seen: that capitalism was not a full-employment system. It was not a system which 'righted' itself, but one which could settle down at high levels of unemployment (as now and in the inter-war years). Keynes's intention was not to change the fundamentals of the system but to overcome what he saw as major defects. He argued that, if unemployed resources existed, the state could expand the economy by increasing demand (which would stimulate output), making investment more profitable. He thought (though with some doubts) that monetary and fiscal measures alone could restore profitability and maintain high levels of employment. It was this view which was repudiated by Jim Callaghan when as Prime Minister he stated at the 1976 Labour Party Conference (the year of capitulation to the International Monetary Fund):

We used to think that you could spend your way out of a recession, and increase employment by cutting taxes and boosting government spending. I tell you in all candour that that option no longer exists, and that in so far as it ever did exist, it only worked . . . by injecting a bigger dose of inflation into the system.

Keynes did believe that a government could spend its way out of a recession. There are problems, however, for capitalist economies if the state does attempt sustained economic growth:

It increases the degree of state intervention in situations where these levers could be used by the labour and socialist movement to threaten the dominance of capital.

It can lead to a nationalized sector which may compete with private firms.

In so far as it contributes to full employment, it strengthens the bargaining power of the trade unions and weakens the reserve army of labour which business likes to have to keep wage costs down and discipline its labour force.

It contributes to the inflationary pressure as firms pass on increased costs in higher prices and the monetary policies of governments accommodate this (on this, Callaghan had a point).

In terms of Keynesian theory, the last thing a government should do, when the economy is depressed and there are large numbers of unemployed and machines idle, is further to deflate the economy. But this is precisely what, for instance, the MacDonald Government did in 1931, the Labour Government did in 1974–9, and Tory Government is doing now. Such deflation makes the crisis worse. The objective, as argued earlier, is to 'knock sense' into the workers, reduce real wages and rationalize capitalist production, with the weaker going to the wall. The way to renewed profitable accumulation is thus opened. The crisis is *used* to rationalize the system; it is a kind of purgative. In these circumstances the fight to expand the economy becomes part of the opposition to big business policies.

Let us return to the argument on economic expansion. If all human and material resources in an economy are being used (well or badly), growth can only take place if productivity rises. In that situation economic policies designed to lift an economy out of crisis will create enormous difficulties in any society.

The proposals that concern us here are intended to lift the economy up towards a state of full employment and secure the basis for continued expansion. We start from a position of around 3 million registered and unregistered unemployed and with much machinery idle for lack of demand.

The need to expand demand is a characteristic emphasis of all supporters of the AES from whatever angle they approach it: increased demand for consumer goods, for public services and for capital equipment. The pressure for increased real post-tax incomes is fully justified in our conditions. I shall argue below that one weakness in the Keynesian view is its belief that fiscal and monetary measures alone are all that are needed to bring about sustained expansion and that investment will follow.

There is a large degree of consensus amongst the supporters of the AES that, apart from increases in real incomes that arise from collective bargaining, the most powerful and desirable way to economic expansion is *a large-scale increase in public spending*, i.e. a total reversal of the principles on which the Tory Government is acting (and for that matter, the Labour Government which preceded it).

Expansion of public spending

What makes this so important and desirable?

First, public spending by central and local government has major public and social advantages because it means, among other things, an expansion of welfare and collective services which can be enjoyed by the great majority of the people whether working or not; it helps the disadvantaged in particular.

Second, the health of the private sector depends on the demand from the public sector and those who work in it. Orders from the public sector and spending by those employed in it constitute an enormous market for private firms, not just in consumer but in investment goods. A major spending programme on housing, health, education, improved buildings and installations means big new orders for private firms as well as nationalized industries (though we are proposing a much wider state-initiated investment programme – see Chapter 5).

Third, the kind of public-spending programme we have so far mentioned has the further advantage that it uses less imports and provides more jobs for any given expenditure. At the moment, for instance, there are well over 300,000 unemployed workers in the construction industry, though Britain is not short of materials such as bricks, cement, concrete, glass, and so on – another reason why increased public spending is initially more helpful than tax cuts in providing more jobs. In such a public-spending programme, Blake and Ormerod (1980)* are right to propose that capital spending should be increased at a much faster rate than current spending given that the former is of course much smaller than the latter.

The argument so far implies that such a public-spending programme, so far from crowding out the private sector, would give it a major boost not only in making more use of existing capacity but inspiring a measure of new investment.

I said earlier that a much *wider* investment programme is needed. Expanding consumer demand is important if the economy is to grow; but it can be argued that the growth-path of an economy will depend on what happens to investment and what kind of investment. Keynes thought that, if the state expanded demand by fiscal and monetary means, firms would respond by increasing investment. But does that necessarily follow? Is there any guarantee that increased demand, stimulated by state spending, will give rise to the *scale* of investment and

---

* See 'Guide to Further Reading' (p. 131) for books referred to in the text.

its *composition* that would meet the needs of the people and the economy in the longer run? We must bear in mind that it is not just the *amount* of investment (though that is important), but where it takes place, in what sectors of the economy, in what areas of technology, and so forth.

We are faced with a *long-run* tendency for British capital to increase its investment and output overseas, and that includes also a great deal of design and technology. All the major multinationals show signs of transferring activities to areas they regard as providing lower costs and political stability. They have no special commitment to most of the regions or countries in which they operate. The great bulk of investment is carried out, aftcr all, by a small number – two to three hundred – of the largest firms.

Given the post-war development of British capitalism, confidence has clearly weakened prospects for growth and profitability of operations in the UK in the long run. Even Mr Heath, whose government made a determined effort to increase domestic demand between 1970 and 1973 was led to complain bitterly as follows:

When we came in we were told there weren't sufficient inducements to invest. So we provided the inducements. Then we were told people were scared of balance of payments difficulties leading to stop-go. So we floated the pound. Then we were told of fears of inflation; and now we're dealing with that. And still you aren't investing enough (Address to the Institute of Directors, quoted in *The Director*, 1973).

I am not arguing that investment no longer responds to economic recovery; it does, but on a limited scale. It is also obvious that the *character* of investment cannot be guaranteed by more consumer expenditure when much of that investment, in high technology for instance, is very risky and needs vast amounts of money at low rates of interest over long periods of time.

The dominant groups of big business and finance have in practice and policy campaigned for deflationary policies by the government of the day, for the reasons we gave earlier. Why should we imagine that a major economic expansion initiated by a government acting under popular and labour movement influence will be met by these groups with open arms? Many will prefer a waiting strategy, building up cash balances, investing in property, and looking for ways of using their funds in sectors and countries where they feel more secure. Many will in any case not be sure that expansion will be sustained long enough to justify the investment, and may even want this to be a self-fulfilling prophecy since it would weaken a government they disliked. Therefore even the limited response of investment to recovery which took place, for instance, in 1972, may not be repeated (and detailed models of the relation between economic upswings and investment based on what happened in the past may be a poor guide).

For these reasons, Keynesian thinking is inadequate.

A government that expanded demand would also face another set of investment problems. These arise from the fact that the level of investment in the past has been low and is currently falling. During 1980 manufacturing investment was estimated to fall by about 10%: a further fall of about 15% (on the reduced figure) is estimated during 1981. Much of the equipment now idle may be obsolete, and much of it is in sectors producing undesired products of poor design or quality. The significance of this is that, with growing demand, the limits of capacity are quickly hit. The goods that people want are not available from British producers; imports would rise swiftly to fill the gap and the consumer boom would run into difficulties. Jobs would not increase proportionately to rising demand because the capacity would not be there.

Yet it is plain that Britain needs a massive investment programme. In that case, if the arguments put earlier have any validity, the state *must* play the major initiating and funding role. As things now stand the fixed investment programmes of the public sector, including the nationalized industries, constitute one third of all fixed investment. But we are talking now of a vast expansion, including the manufacturing sector.

In manufacturing, for instance, investment per head would need to be *doubled* to bring us up to the level of West Germany. A reasonable aim would be to increase manufacturing investment by about 25% over the 1979 level within three or four years. Large investment programmes are needed for energy and conservation; the railways need to invest between £300 and £400 millions to maintain an up-to-date system; and communications and aerospace involve massive investment spending. In addition, the revolution in information and automation requires major research and development spending in areas like microelectronics, lasers and fibre optics, biotechnologies and energy-related technologies. Moreover, an integral part of such an investment programme is a major development of the education and training system. Industrial training alone requires *twice* the £1,000 million now spent by industry and government.

This is hardly an exhaustive list but even so suggests the large-scale investment that needs to be planned and developed *over many years*. And it must be added to the capital spending on welfare and allied central and local government services.

This is a different perspective to increasing state aid to prop up 'lame ducks' without tackling the causes of British industry's long-run problems.

Not that the state alone can carry through all of this investment programme. It could not and it should not. It must involve a combined effort of central and local government, the nationalized industries, and the large private firms; but ways must also be found of stimulating investment by small and medium-sized firms (see Chapter 5).

How?

Large-scale state intervention in manufacturing will powerfully affect private investment because it will determine the amount and types of investment goods demanded from private firms; it can increase the share of manufacturing in national output and increase its total amount as well. Using its own large-scale model, the Cambridge Growth Project has tried to measure the effects of an ambitious investment programme (one quarter higher than in 1979), and estimated that growth rate would rise to just over 3%, the rate of inflation would be cut to under 10%, and 600,000 new jobs would be created; the share of manufacturing would be kept at 28% of GDP, and GDP itself would rise in real terms by nearly 40% by 1990 over its 1976 level (*Guardian*, 18/8/1980).

How could such an investment programme be financed?

In the first place, economic growth to some degree finances itself as unemployment falls and output and income rise; industries become more profitable and government revenues increase.

Second, the financial resources that exist and come into existence can be used more efficiently and be better directed (see Chapter 5).

But there is a third source: the growing revenues from North Sea oil which on some estimates will rise to about 9 billion pounds (in 1980 prices) by 1985. Even if government left the present ownership of North Sea oil as it is (which it should not!), the use of those revenues – amounting to far more than the total spent on manufacturing investment in the UK – would help transform the industrial base of Britain.

These funds could be invested at low rates of interest so that a long-term view can be taken in place of the short-sighted, swift-pay-back attitudes that now dominate the thinking of large numbers of firms.

Put briefly, the argument so far has been that an expansion programme is necessary and possible; it requires decisive state intervention especially in the field of investment, and it can be financed. But there are also problems. One of them, which is the certainty that rising incomes would also bring even more rapidly rising imports, is dealt with in Chapter 6. In the rest of this chapter I want to take up the other two. The first of these is employment, the second is inflation.

Can we get back to full employment?

To get back to full employment, by which most people mean reducing unemployment to the 2 to 300,000 of the 1950s, is a key objective of all plans for expansion. But the fact remains that none of the plans so far put forward, and which attempt to work out in detail the effect on employment, are able to do better than get the unemployed down to about 700,000 over a period of years. Economic expansion will go part of the way to getting more jobs. But no less a problem is the speed with which such programmes could produce jobs. The more one examines the problem the clearer it is that even to get down to 700,000 requires a whole series of emergency and longer-term measures. It is impossible to say how many unemployed there need to be to have 'full employment', but we could argue that it would be less than 700,000 on the basis of past experience.

The overall unemployment figures were given in Chapter 2 but we need to look at them in more detail.

If we try to take account of seasonal influences, the number of registered adults unemployed in December 1980 was 2,133,000, plus 170,000 school-leavers, making a total of 2,244,000. This figure excluded those temporarily suspended. More important, it excluded those who wanted jobs but who were not registered (women, for instance, looking for part-time work who found that there was no point in registering). That number could have been of the order of 400,000. The combined figure was 2,644,000 despite government schemes which kept about 250,000 off the register.

Within this vast body there was a growing core of *long-term* unemployed; one third were on the register for more than six months. In general, the unskilled were hit harder than the skilled, part-time more than full-time workers. Young, especially black, people and women were disproportionately affected.

Between January and July 1980, *notified* redundancies were about a quarter of a million and vacancies notified were down by half in a year.

Total employment in manufacturing fell by 400,000 in the six months to June 1980, and numbers began to fall also in the service sector which was no longer growing to take up the slack.

In addition about 300,000 were working short time which, for many, proved to be the prelude to losing their jobs. And we must note the big differences between the regions, with unemployment figures in Scotland, Wales, Northern Ireland, and the North well above the national average.

If present policies continue the prospects are very grim, as everyone now knows. Some estimates suggest registered unemployment rising to 3 million; the Cambridge *Economic Policy Review* has spoken of 5 million by 1985 as possible. Youth unemployment is likely to be nearly half a million by the end of 1981.

The costs of unemployment are large and wide ranging. In terms of cost to government, every newly-unemployed person means additional public sector borrowing of £5,000. The October 1980 level of unemployment involved government borrowing of about £7,000 million. Unemployment costs Britain around £10 billion in lost production and services.

There are also social costs which are harder to calculate but real: the rise in physical and mental ill-health, and increased vandalism and petty crime. One estimate suggests that a rise in unemployment of one million could, over five years, lead to 50,000 more deaths, over 60,000 cases of mental illness and 14,000 more people receiving prison sentences (Rowthorn and Ward, quoted in the *Financial Times*, 18/8/80). During August 1980, the Samaritans in North-East England found a sharp rise in suicide calls from young unemployed people.

Before saying why special measures are needed, the question is sometimes put whether we are not obsessed by the importance of work. It is true that people can benefit from and increasingly learn more effectively to use greater leisure to diversify their activities. But not if they are poor and believe themselves to be society's rejects. As things are now and are likely to be for a considerable time, to have a job, to earn one's keep, to establish one's worth amongst workmates, to acquire and use skills and abilities, to advance in one's work, is important for self-esteem and sense of purpose. On this, all surveys of those out of work are clear. An advanced industrial society that cannot offer that to at least 95% of its labour force is doing material and moral damage.

What are the difficulties in cutting unemployment to half a million in a short period, even with an expansion programme?

First, a great deal more manufacturing output can come from existing capacity and workforce without any corresponding increase in jobs.

Second, to the extent that productivity rises as fast as increased output, no new jobs are created; if it rises faster, there could be fewer jobs. The results of a big investment programme therefore may be not many more or fewer jobs.

Third, in sectors which have been very labour intensive such as services of all kinds, the new information revolution (based on microelectronics) could reduce jobs, especially in banking and insurance, process industries, printing and publishing, education, health services, retailing and transport operations. Clerical jobs of all kinds would be most at risk. Even if forecasts have been over-pessimistic, employment in some areas is bound to be affected and the number of *new* jobs created by technical change is difficult to estimate.

Fourth, and at the present time the most important factor apart from the depression and government policy, is the increase taking place in the labour force. Between 1978 and 1985 the population of working age will have increased by 1·15 million and, because more women will look for work, the workforce will rise by 1·3 million. So it is not just a question of finding work for those now unemployed, but of creating large numbers of new jobs for those entering the labour force. Over half a million new jobs would have to be created by 1982 just to absorb such new entrants. So, as we have seen, the prospects for young people in particular are bad.

Finally there is the real problem of whether the kind of skilled labour needed by such a programme is available in the relevant places. The way industry is distributed between regions cannot be swiftly changed.

The Cambridge Growth Project plans would create 600,000 new jobs but still leave unemployment over the million. The Cambridge Economic Policy Group proposals would leave unemployment at 1·8 million in 1985 and only reduce it to 1·3 million in 1990. So it is obvious that a whole battery of measures are needed, both emergency and long-term.

The expansion programme outlined earlier does of course mean many new jobs in labour intensive services, such as health, education and welfare, and in scientific and professional services generally. Rising real incomes will expand the demand for private as well as public services of all kinds. What is needed in addition?

First, there is a powerful argument for large-scale temporary employment subsidies. Tom Sheriff for instance (in Blake and Ormerod, 1980) proposed £40 a week to employers who take on extra workers whom they could demonstrate they would otherwise not take on. Estimates suggest that £500 million used in this way would save or create 250,000 jobs.

Second, the use of a whole series of emergency schemes should be considered, especially for young people, involving extension of the Youth Opportunity Programmes, and other measures, as advocated for instance by the TUC General Council in October 1980.

Third, there should be faster progress towards the 35-hour week and reductions in overtime. Sometimes the calculations made exaggerate the number of jobs that would be thus created; it is not without costs but, within an expansionary programme, it could make a large contribution (see Appendix).

Fourth, and exceptionally important in short and long term, a major new education and training programming should be provided for both the young and the retraining of older people. It is astonishing that the UK has only 100,000 apprenticeships while West Germany has many times that number. Even now, in an economic crisis, the Sector Working Party for Automation and Instrumentation (set up by the National Economic Development Office) complained that skill shortages are regarded as severe enough to cause reduced output and the postponement of investment and development plans.

Fifth, employers must be made to enter into genuine negotiations over introducing new technology. In the transition to an expansionary programme in which employees can feel secure, overmanning is not a crime: unemployment is.

These are suggestions which taken together with the general programme for economic growth can increase employment over time very substantially as shown in the Appendix. Some of them could be introduced now if public pressure were strong enough, and this would help the fight for more extensive measures and indeed for a new strategy. From which arises the second of the major problems: inflation.

Won't a major expansion programme make inflation worse? *Isn't the reduction in inflation the most important precondition for growth?*

Inflation
The Tory Government (like its Labour predecessor) presents inflation as the central problem of the British economy, and the reduction in the rate of inflation as the central aim to which everything must be subor-

dinated at whatever cost. This is a complete misunderstanding of what has gone wrong with the economy, and policies based on such a view are bound to be damaging. The key to our difficulties is the systematic neglect of Britain's productive base which has proceeded through periods of boom and slump, inflation and deflation and indeed through periods, as now, of stagflation. This is rooted in the way in which British capitalism has developed and is the outcome of the strategies adopted.

The fact that British inflation is so much higher than most, if not all, of our major rivals is a *symptom* of this relative decline and low growth in conditions where a severe conflict over resources has taken place.

Inflation is a problem for three important reasons. One is that, when prices not merely rise but go up at an *increasing rate*, powerful anxieties are created amongst all economic agents; there is a fear that money will become worthless, and people with resources begin to convert money into gold, property or other 'real' assets. The entire process of economic activity seems to be in danger. Another reason is that inflation tends to redistribute resources from lenders to borrowers as interest rates lag behind rising price. The main beneficiaries of this are government and companies, both generally net borrowers. It also redistributes between people on fixed incomes and those able to keep up with rising prices (house-owners as against tenants, etc.). This also sets up many tensions. A third reason is that, if prices in Britain rise faster than they do in other countries, the rate of exchange is affected. If the pound falls imports will become dearer, the cost of living will rise, and pressure for money wages to compensate will be hard to resist. Rising costs and rising prices move into an upward spiral.

These reasons are not trivial; inflation is a real problem. But before saying what should be done about it, we have to ask whether the reasons given above fully explain why the Tory Government has made inflation the central issue of policy. Because it latches onto a real concern of people, inflation has proved a mighty battering-ram in the battle of ideas.

To a large degree (though not entirely) the belief that the most important task is to reduce inflation is sincerely held, and there are good *class* reasons why. As I suggested earlier, the state-supported growth policies of post-war governments, committed to full employment, had in them the seed of future difficulties, inflation amongst them. But the argument that inflation is *central* is linked with the argument that its main cause is trade union pressure for higher wages which outstrip productivity. With this argument the entire weight of the major problems of the economy can be placed on the unions. It justifies the view that we have been paying ourselves more than we earn, and that public spending and other sources of 'excess' demand must be cut, even if this means large-scale unemployment. And in so far as the monetarist view is upheld, the money supply is to be squeezed so that workers must choose between more money (if their employers can afford it), or jobs.

To some extent this is ground we have already covered in the previous chapter. There too we examined what was being done in the name of fighting inflation. The outcome, as we have seen, has been *inflation combined with deflation*. But, and it is an important but, the significance of the inflation argument is that it focuses on what the employers and the Tories regard as central — the drive to cut wage costs and weaken the bargaining power of the unions. They repudiate Keynesianism because they believe it has been responsible for assisting in the creation of a powerful counterforce.

Any serious alternative economic strategy must say what it would like to do about prices; but — though this might shock some readers — an economy can live and live quite well with *some* degree of inflation *providing* it is not allowed to accelerate and providing other measures are carried through. The experience of countries like Sweden shows that an efficient capitalist economy can have virtual full employment, a low rate of inflation, and yet also have levels of public spending far greater than the UK even before Mrs Thatcher's cuts.

The causes of inflation have been and look like remaining the subject of intense debate amongst economists for a long time. The attempt to find a single primal cause is misplaced, whether it be the change in the money supply argued by Milton Friedman or the wage-push thesis argued by others. The proposition that inflation arises where workers, capitalists and governments try to satisfy conflicting claims in conditions in which credit expands well ahead of output offers a more useful framework. Capitalists trying to improve or maintain profit margins, trade unionists trying to maintain or improve real wages, governments trying to carry through their spending plans — all in a situation of low growth and low productivity — create the conditions for an inflationary spiral. It is not necessary to know of some 'first cause' to do something about it. What should be quite clear from our earlier arguments is that the worst solution to be attempted from the standpoint of the majority of people is savage deflation.

The reason why an expansionary strategy is more sensible is that, whereas deflation means falling output and falling productivity, expansion means rising output and rising productivity. That in turn can prevent or moderate any rise in unit costs and subsequently in prices. Further, a growth strategy, by producing more goods and services, begins to meet people's expectations; real incomes can rise and provide a different framework for wage bargaining.

But expansion alone will not prevent, under British conditions, some rise in prices. Apart from wage bargaining itself, which I shall come to in a moment, there are two other kinds of action that will be important.

In the area of fiscal and monetary policy, the increases in indirect taxes which put up the retail price index would be reversed. VAT should be cut with sharper distinctions between basic goods and luxury goods. Nationalized industries should have access to funds on terms which do not oblige them to push up their prices to almost suicidal levels (like, for instance, the vicious spiral of rising fares and falling income in the railways). A lower rate of interest would obviously help to reduce pressure on price levels.

But in addition, to show its determination to break the spiral of rising prices, some measure of price control is indispensable for a government that wants its strategy to be taken seriously by the mass of people. Price control *can* be effective; it has been used with some success at different times in such countries as France, and for that matter in Britain itself when the Price Code was being seriously applied. Its success partly depends on an expanding economy so that firms find their unit costs falling and price control does not severely squeeze their pre-tax profits. The profits will be there but they will arise from more efficient and increased output. A price control system would have to have considerable flexibility and will inevitably become a major source of information and control on the pricing policies of at least the major firms. Pricing policy is a key element in the strategy of firms and cannot be separated from their investment plans and how they propose to finance them. That is why pricing has to be an integral part of the proposed planning agreements (discussed in the following chapter) between the government and the major enterprises (public and private). However, I would not like to give the impression that it is possible or sensible to freeze prices in any economy for any long period of time. There is only too much experience from capitalist and socialist countries to show that prices must take account of changing conditions, in demand, relative productivity, competition from alternative or substitute goods, and so on. But price control remains an indispensable instrument and at a particular moment can create confidence in a measure of price stability.

Wages and wage bargaining

What then of wages and wage bargaining, the issue which has been at the centre of public debate?

To the employer wages are a cost along with other costs and therefore are significant for the way prices are determined. Obviously their significance varies from sector to sector. In capital-intensive industries, such as oil refining, their share is small; in labour-intensive sectors, such as transport and services, it is large. But such a statement is only the *beginning* of the story. What is important to the employer are costs per unit of output including *wage costs* per unit of output.

However, the latter does not depend only on the level of earnings, but even more on the technology employed, the efficiency with which the labour and production process is organized and whether the productive capacity is being used or under-used. Earnings will therefore be only one element in determining the cost per unit of output, though it may be more important in some industries than in others. How workers and unions behave has some influence on technology and efficiency but for the most part hardly a crucial one: it has very little influence indeed on whether capacity is fully used or not, because workers and unions do not control the way the economy behaves.

From the workers' standpoint the standard of living depends, among other things, on the bundle of goods and services which post-tax wages can buy. At this level the policies followed by governments which affect taxes and prices become very critical.

Moreover, even when costs have been determined by all these factors, the price still also depends upon the profit margin which firms decide is possible given the conditions under which they operate.

So the wage bargain is important, but its significance for prices depends on the conditions under which it is struck. Since trade unions do not *control* these conditions they must bargain and negotiate with employers and government.

Whatever debate there may be about the phrase 'free' or 'normal' collective bargaining, the principle at stake is whether trade unions should be independent, autonomous bodies seeking to advance the interests of their members in the wisest way they know and be responsive to them, i.e. genuinely democratic in their functioning. This principle is being established the hard way in both capitalist and socialist economies.

The experience of so-called incomes policies from the late forties onwards has been associated with attempts to cut real wages without any serious changes in class and social relationships. Not surprisingly, both Labour and Tory governments have foundered in the attempt to maintain such policies beyond the support of major sections of workers.

None of this can possibly mean that trade unions have no responsibility for what happens in the economy or that they do not need to formulate a wage strategy.

Any government in Britain pledged to expand the economy, restore high levels of employment, and initiate far-reaching democratization of economic, social and political life could only come into existence with the active support and campaigning of the bulk of the trade union movement. It would not be a government imposed on or independent of the wishes of the 12 million trade unionists and their families.

For this reason the bargaining process must take into account the overall direction of the economy. But it has to do this with full democratic accountability to the membership of the unions. There is experience to show that trade union pressure for rising living standards is a vital check on arbitrary decisions and gross errors in investment and other policies. The independence of the unions and their readiness to defend workers' conditions would help to ensure that government economic policies are not out of line with the aspirations of the labour force itself.

The level and rate of increase of wages is inevitably a crucial economic and political issue for governments – of whatever political complexion – in all modern economies. This is because they are major employers and also because of the effects of wages on the economy as a whole. Any government will have a wage policy of its own; and certainly a left government, on popular insistence, would be concerned with the distribution of resources between consumption and investment, and between classes and groups, as well as with the labour supply and such factors as the effects of differentials.

As matters now stand, the trade union movement requires to develop a progressive wage policy of its own which tries to take care of the unity and long-term interests of working people as a whole. Everyone is aware of sectional and sometimes competing interests: between workers in the private and public sectors, between service and manufacturing sectors, between white and blue-collar workers, between men and women workers, between established workers and new entrants to the labour market. Technological change itself sets up many disturbances as events in the shipbuilding and printing industry have shown (to mention only two of many examples).

Such a wage policy must take account of the demand for a minimum wage, equal pay for work of equal value, and some code for handling issues of differentials and job possibilities. It must begin to look at the bargaining process, not just from the standpoint of male workers but of the millions of women workers who are often also housewives and mothers. It must concern itself with workers who have no industrial 'muscle' as well as with those who have. Discriminations against workers (e.g. women and black workers) is one of the crucial problems of the eighties.

But a trade union backed wages policy must do more than this. As the main force of organized workers in Britain, trade union concern for the millions of people *not* in unions must go beyond the passing of resolutions. Nearly half of male workers and three fifths of women workers are not in unions. There are hundreds of thousands of school-leavers with no experience at all of trade unions, and large numbers of unemployed who worked in badly-organized sectors of the economy. Beyond these again, there must be concern for the millions who are not in the labour force at all – for housewives and mothers at home, and for pensioners and the young. This can be done by the unions in collaboration with the Labour Party, the Communist Party, the Co-operative movement, other labour and socialist parties and groups, and with the many organizations of feminists, ethnic minorities and pressure groups.

The formation of such wide-ranging and constructive policies by the unions, and the campaign for them, are vital if the unions are to break through the ghetto in which the Tory Government is trying to confine them.

It may seem that this discussion on the trade unions has taken us beyond the theme of expanding the economy. But growth is a means not an end. The objectives are improved services, rising real living standards, and greater efficiency so that resources and time can be released for leisure and personal development. And the kind of expansion with which this book is concerned only has meaning if the force that powers it is that of working people and their families.

5 Power and the People: Is Democratic Control of the Economy Possible?

By democratic control we mean the ability of people organized in their political parties, trade unions, consumer organizations, community and interest groups – through representative bodies and ad hoc pressure groups – to take part in the formulation and carrying through of economic policy. What is the case for it?

One argument stands out plainly from what has already been said: Toryism and big business want to resolve the problems of the economy in the way that suits their interests and on their terms. They have in mind a tighter, more rationalized capitalism which will severely weaken all the forces of resistance, so that recovery when it comes will be all the more profitable for the survivors. The crisis will have knocked out much 'excess capacity', led to the writing down of the value of large amounts of capital, and the transfer of much of it to other capitalists, who, having acquired it more cheaply, believe they can use it more profitably.

This is an entirely different solution to the one which is sought by the AES. Our programme is for economic expansion as against the deflationary policies of the present government. But that is only a starting point. What is no less important is *how* that expansion takes place, in *which* directions, and *who* are to benefit. Popular and democratic intervention is the only force which can both reverse current policies and impose a new direction on the economy.

But there is a further argument for democratic control: that it is a basic human right for people to be involved in decisions and actions which concern them. This is part of a democratic struggle which has gone on for a long time and has now become particularly intense because of the powerful forces at work to throw back even existing limited degrees of democratic influence.

Within the labour movement itself there are sectarian groups who believe that the economic crisis is a problem for the capitalist to solve and that workers have no concern with practical proposals because, it is argued, these amount to managing capitalism for the capitalists. There are also those who take a narrow and 'non-political' view, arguing that unions exist simply to improve wages and conditions and are not concerned with wider issues of government policy. The significance of the AES is that it proposes practical interventions in economic policy which would advance the interests of the people and *extend*, and not simply protect, democratic controls. In essence, these interventions are part of a struggle for power.

If it was not understood before, an economic crisis brings home the fact that economic power is real. Here is a check list: who decides what is produced? how it's produced? where it's produced? at what price? drawing on whose inputs? selling in which markets? how the surplus is used?

Such decisions, taken by the two hundred largest firms in Britain, decide which regions (if any) prosper and which decay; where there is work and where there is unemployment; which cities and boroughs have resources and which have none; which industries thrive and which are eliminated; how much is spent on training; how much on research and development? And so on.

The concentration of such economic power involves political power. To maintain the profitable accumulation of firms becomes a vital concern of government and determines a large part of the activities of the state. The concentration of wealth is in the hands of a social group which monopolizes privileged education and occupies a disproportionate number of the top positions in the machinery of state. The interlocking of top civil servants and big business and the exchange of personnel has become very plain. In the case of the Tory Party the linkages between big finance and industry are direct and personal.

That same concentrated wealth operates in the mass media, especially in the press and in independent television, and exerts unceasing pressure on the BBC (quite apart from the extent to which values are shared between them).

If all this is true, then the *idea that we can get sustained economic growth in the interests of the people and under their control without changes in the social and property relationships is an illusion.*

How to change these power relationships is, in the final analysis, the fundamental problem and it is the recognition of this which is the great strength of Marxist socialism. Chapter 9 discusses overall strategy in some detail; this chapter considers what kind of transfer of power from big business is needed to carry out the main objectives of the AES.

A shift in power as radical as the one presented in this chapter can only be implemented by a government of the left backed by overwhelming public support. It assumes the existence of a powerful and mounting struggle in which the organizations of the labour and trade union movement, working together with many other movements and streams of opinion, become involved in a wide-ranging debate on policy; and that these forces reach a measure of agreement reflected in the programme of a government of the left.

These are the conditions necessary to ensure that the democratic process will in the lifetime of such a government be capable of formulating policy objectives and secure popular support, for both the proposed direction of the economy and the means by which the changes are to be made.

It is here that many of the most difficult questions arise, including those of public ownership and planning and their compatibility with the involvement of people. The questions of ownership, control, accountability and planning cannot be evaded. But to do what? and with what degree of power? and who is to excercise it and how?

Why is planning an important issue?

The idea of planning has been a dirty word especially since the collapse of the National Plan put forward by the Labour Government in 1965. An enormous effort has been made by the Tories, business circles and the media to discredit the very concept. For others, especially on the left, planning has been a magic word which can cure all problems and which, in an unfortunate way, has been identified with socialism. Planning in fact can solve some problems and cause others; it has a variety of interpretations and possible practices. Varying degrees of it are compatible with different types of capitalist and socialist societies.

Control of the economy is of course inseparable from the intervention of central government and of the state. As we showed in earlier chapters, the Tories have been able to make effective use of the widespread feeling that state intervention and state ownership represent rampant and insensitive bureaucracy. Their critique is completely hypocritical: the large capitalist firms are often extremely bureaucratic and despotic. Moreover, an increasing number of the Tory Government's measures represent restrictions on individual rights and on the ability of groups of people to influence policy, its determined undermining of local government autonomy is one of the strongest illustrations of this.

Governments, whether Labour or Tory, have no choice but to form an overview of the requirements (as they understand them) of the economy and the direction in which they wish it to move. They establish some set of social criteria. They are involved in far-reaching decisions both over large-scale investment (such as nuclear energy) and government spending and taxation.

Governments have also to take into account that large firms and financial institutions carry out full-scale planning within their own organizations and often control subordinate areas which supply them with inputs or take their outputs. The scale of these enterprises means that they are effectively planning substantial slices of the economy. Moreover, sometimes with government encouragement, they co-ordinate their activities in allocating markets and fixing prices.

Governments do not face something called a 'free market economy' – that is a myth. They are themselves major forces in the economy and they deal with giant firms engaged in varying mixtures of rivalry and collusion.

To apply the kind of package discussed in Chapter 4, a left government must be deeply involved in a number of crucial macroeconomic decisions. Amongst the most important are large-scale investment decisions especially in the following areas: in the infrastructure, energy, transport, and housing, including where that investment is to take place; in key areas of manufacturing, especially concerning high technology and research and development in intensive industries; in welfare, social services and defence.

In turn these must mean decisions about the allocation of resources, e.g. the proportion devoted to investment as compared with consumption, priority areas, and consequently also fiscal and monetary policies, as well as some degree of physical planning.

It ought to be clear from our description of the root problems of the British economy that, in our conditions, the government formed by the democratically-elected party must take responsibility for these decisions. In some of these areas it already does, but in manufacturing industry for instance, the decisions cannot be simply left – as they in practice often are – to individual firms. Firms may not want to take the risks involved; they may not have the resources; they may prefer not to invest on such a scale in case their rivals retaliate in some way; they may not consider the likely profits sufficiently tempting; they may have alternative uses for their funds in other sectors and other countries; they may be hostile to the intentions of the government. Firms cannot balance the social and private costs and benefits; the outcome of many individual decisions may be completely the reverse of the common interest.

If a left government is to be able to take these decisions on the basis of a democratically agreed perspective, what is necessary?

First, it will need some additional degree of public ownership, but (see Section II below) set up on a different and more democratic basis than hitherto. Second, it must create a legal-political-economic framework within which there can be public accountability of the giant industrial and financial enterprises, and collaboration between public and private firms and organizations.

That framework should include a major expansion of cooperative and local authority-sponsored enterprises, and a variety of different ways of allowing the small and medium firms (and the self-employed) to cooperate and develop. The administrative convenience of dealing with large units should not blind us to the importance of small and medium-scale enterprises (*public*, private and cooperative) which, because of modern technology in production and communication, can often be very efficient.

We have (and so also have socialist countries) bitter experience to prove that state ownership in itself may have few virtues; it may be necessary in certain areas but it is never sufficient even to guarantee co-ordination, still less the public interest. This depends on policy, personnel and popular involvement.

What kind of planning?

As I have shown, we do not live in a 'free market economy'. Some degree of planning exists in all modern economies; the very idea that the choice is between a 'free market economy' and an economy planned in detail from a single centre involves a false antithesis. There have indeed been illusions that such total centralized planning is possible, but systems of planning which have attempted it have run into major difficulties. The justification has sometimes been that a backward economy, needing to make swift and dramatic changes, must harness all its resources behind certain major decisions, at whatever cost elsewhere (for instance, if a country is at war).

However, in advanced capitalist economies this justification does not exist; in any case it is wrong in principle and impossible in practice. It is wrong in principle because no group of central planners, however appointed, *should* be given the power to decide in complete detail what is to happen to an economy with all its social implications.

It is impossible in practice for at least four reasons. First, because central planners (or anyone else) cannot know the future, or the actual resources and potentialities of each economic unit – there is always a degree of unavoidable ignorance. Second, modern economies are incredibly complex; they function by way of densely interwoven webs of transactions and adjustments which makes it impossible to know the effects of making changes on other parts of the system. Third, no central body, even the most dictatorial, can possess the power to control and direct what everyone does in the economy. Fourth, it cannot adequately analyse and process the information it needs in order to take the immense number of decisions.

Since this is not a book about a future socialist economy I do not need to set out a blueprint on how it would work, even if one were available. Nevertheless, ideas about what should be done by a government of the left are inevitably shaped by the longer-run perspective, so it is necessary to say something about it. In this 'model' the central government, together with local authorities and national assemblies, would concern itself with a limited number of crucial national macroeconomic decisions: the shares of investment, personal and collective consumption; the distribution of income; major investment decisions which shape the direction of the economy over long periods of time; and regional policies.

Enterprises would operate on a basis of a code of conduct on which central government would, through consultation, exercise certain critical influences, such as on the rate of interest and on the rate of taxation. Apart from that, enterprises would produce, buy and sell from each other and to the public on the basis of normal negotiations and patterns of demand. Individuals would decide for themselves how to spend their post-tax incomes, and where they would work, and would expect enterprises to respond to their needs.

In this sense 'the market' and the 'price mechanism' would play an important role. This will limit the need for bureaucratic decision-making; it avoids making every economic decision a directly political one for some meeting or body formally to discuss and decide; it makes it easier for small-scale enterprises to function. Moreover, through the need of enterprises to supply what is demanded, competition stimulates innovation and responsiveness. That means establishing an industrial structure which does not allow enterprises to act as monopolists (which can happen even if the workers in those enterprises run them in a completely democratic way). Such a model learns from the experiences – negative and positive – of existing planned economies and is the *direction* in which we should move.*

It will be obvious that the broad approach presented earlier about the areas of decision for a left government, the degree of public ownership, the framework for accountability, control and collaboration with the private sector, can be seen as a step towards such a model, but it is not *dependent* on acceptance of it.

In the rest of this chapter I attempt to follow through the argument by dealing with the extension of public ownership that seems to be necessary, the methods of establishing accountability and control of the major enterprises and harnessing their resources, the specific problem of dealing with the multinationals, the mechanisms of democratic planning, and the issue of industrial democracy.

II EXTENDING THE PUBLIC SECTOR

In the previous section I put forward the unwillingness or inability of privately-owned firms to make major investment decisions and/or provide vital services for the economy and society as a whole as an obvious justification for an extension of public ownership. But there is another reason which has played a big part in the labour movement's traditional demand for nationalization: the view that public ownership would mean an extension of democratic control over the economy, removing centres of economic power from private capital.

That reason is still important, but it has been undermined by the actual practice of nationalization. To restore belief in nationalization means that a left government cannot re-establish or extend public ownership on the model of the present day 'public corporations'. Unless industrial democracy is built into them, their employees and clients will feel no less alienated. In fact, unless this is the conception put forward now, no government is likely to have a mandate to take over firms or industries except under pressure of bankruptcy.

The third reason for extending public ownership is that enterprises under some measure of central control are more easily coordinated,

* This 'model' is not put forward as an ideal system, only as a stage in a much longer process in which people learn to cooperate in unselfish and creative ways.

more amenable to rules framed in the public interest, if the will is there and if the personnel who direct them share objectives.

Public ownership in the form of state-owned enterprises is of course only one form of social ownership. There are other forms, such as co-operatives, and consortiums owned and controlled by local authorities. However, my primary preoccupation in this section is with those crucial areas necessary for sustained expansion not amenable to anything but large-scale planning. The proposals presented are limited in scope; even if they were carried through, the bulk of manufacturing, trading and agriculture and what are now currently non-public services (opticians, etc.) would, as we shall see, still be in private hands. Even so, these proposals threaten important sources of power and profit for big business and will meet intense opposition. But that is no reason for dodging the issue.

There are three critical areas in which decisions to extend public ownership are important for any left government wishing to implement a new strategy.

First, the main infrastructure: energy, transport, and the construction industry; second, key sectors of investment goods and high technology; third, major financial institutions which channel internal and external flows of funds.

I shall discuss each in turn briefly, but the discussion must take account of the difference between taking an entire sector into public ownership (i.e. including the activities in a given sector of all the firms that operate in it) and acquiring one or more firms within a sector. In general, large firms tend to operate in many industries and many countries so the issues that arise are very complex. For these reasons there is unlikely to be a similar answer in each area; but my concern here is with the main thrust of policy and not with detailed plans or comprehensive lists of proposals.

The main infrastructure: energy, transport and the construction industry

Because an economy's infrastructure is so vital to its ability to function and because it is in this area that private capital in Britain has failed to provide the services required, ownership by central and local government is already well established. Reversing Tory action to hand parts back to private ownership (or to offer private capital a stake, etc.), the main extensions necessary are in energy, transport and construction.

The importance of *energy* badly needs debate. We want everyone to be able to meet their basic energy needs at prices they can afford; for industry to be provided with energy based on resource-cost and long-run availability; and for more research on and development of renewable resources, environmental needs and – exceptionally important – effective conservation.

The energy situation is one that cries out for a coordinated national strategy. Britain has bitter experience of letting the market decide when the mining industry was run down, creating an excessive dependence on imported oil and stampeding opinion into a large-scale, costly nuclear energy programme. At the moment the important government stake in North Sea oil (through BNOC) is under attack. Britain has coal, natural gas and oil, and the capacity for a nuclear programme. Coal, gas and electricity are already state owned. The most important extension is to *place all North Sea oil into public ownership.* BNOC at the moment owns about 60% of North Sea crude oil in cash or kind and controls about 35% of production. This means acquiring the interests in North Sea oil of BP, Shell and Burmah oil companies and of about 25 major American companies.

The view that North Sea oil is a public asset to be exploited in the interests of Britain is not just a view on the left but is shared by many other circles in politics, industry and finance. With such an extension the use of North Sea oil and gas can be effectively coordinated as part of a national energy programme; the enormous and growing revenues would be at the disposal of the economy; less would flow back to foreign oil companies, though some may work under service contracts as required. The use of those revenues is critical, as we suggested in the previous chapter, for financing the major new investment plans needed to revitalize British industry.

Is there not a case also for full public ownership of BP (in which the state still holds 46% of the shares), and of the UK operations of Shell? The consequences go beyond the production of oil but extend into refining and petrochemicals. The proposed gas pipe-line should also be publicly owned. Acquiring these firms raises the major question of the massive assets, owned by BP, for instance, in other countries, an issue which needs thorough discussion.

Perhaps in no other areas is the need for a coordinated policy so plain as in *transport*. As a result of pressure to operate as a commercial concern the railway system has suffered dismantlement in many areas; it has been starved of investment and pushed into a vicious cycle of rising fares and fewer passengers. More commuters have thus been forced on to the roads; destructive competition has been encouraged by denationalizing road haulage, and juggernauts and road schemes have been disproportionately encouraged and expanded. Public transport is a vital social service; it makes sense therefore to reunite road and rail transport under public ownership, including the bulk of private long-distance road haulage.

Concern with housing and the need to end casual labour has under-pinned the labour movement's traditional pressure for increased public control of the *construction industry*. Cuts in public spending have led to a severe fall in new house building, and the effect of the recession and high interest rates on investment has led to a situation where well over 350,000 building workers are unemployed. Between 1967 and 1977, output in construction fell by 1·3% per year – in an industry which in 1975 accounted for nearly one fifth of total industrial output and employed.

Private builders have inflicted heavy losses on local authorities all over Britain. However, nationalization of the building industry is not the issue. By far the most important step to be taken is to extend and strengthen direct labour organizations by local authorities as against the current trend to cut them back. They should be allowed to compete for any construction work, public or private, in their area.

For everyday repair and improvement, especially bearing in mind that more than half of all homes (nearly 60%) are now owner-occupied, the many thousands of small builders, most working on their own account, have a key role to play and should be encouraged to form co-operatives and consortiums to improve their services.

To sum up: major public control and extended ownership of energy and transport, and an increased influence in construction would make a planned and coordinated strategy easier to achieve. It would make it possible to maintain an independent energy supply, provide large sums for new investment and limit the outflow of North Sea oil profits to the USA. It would make it possible to regenerate the large city centres and revive parts of the country affected by the cuts in public transport, where the scale and urgency of the need for coordinated strategies cannot be carried through without public ownership.

Key sectors of investment goods and high technology

If we look at nationalization since 1945 we can see that it mostly con-cerned the service industries, such as coal, gas, electricity, railways, and road haulage. Steel was the exception and it was bitterly fought over.

The manufacturing industries and firms that were later acquired would otherwise have collapsed, such as British Leyland, Rolls-Royce, and major shipbuilding firms. In general, the giant firms in manufacturing, trade and finance had no intention of surrendering to public ownership, though they were not hostile to state funds. Enormous sums of public money have gone into rebuilding and modernizing these major state-owned service industries and preventing other firms or sectors from collapsing. But manufacturing industry in Britain has not distinguished itself by its innovation or investment. It is low down in the league of spending on research and development, and sluggish in adopting new technologies.

Any attempt by a left government to stimulate a major investment programme based on the most modern technology and innovations must involve intervention in a number of critical areas of manufacture. These include electronics, computing and electrical engineering; aerospace; machine tools; special steels and tubes, petrochemicals and chemicals; and more general support for high technology areas and research and development. Financing large-scale investment, research and development does not necessarily involve taking over firms or industries unless they have shown total incapacity to respond. Such proposals as the nationalization of the 250 largest firms in manufacturing and trade would represent a massive revolutionary act which would have insignificant support, would maximize hostility to the government, and is unnecessary for the kind of changes this book proposes.

Nevertheless, there are firms in these key areas which, for various reasons, are candidates for public ownership. In electrical and heavy engineering, for instance, GEC, the major force in that sector, and beneficiary of defence contracts, has shown itself to be a skilful rationalizer but poor in innovation and investment. Indeed it has held back from new investment in the UK, preferring to build up massive cash balances to be used for acquisitions both here and overseas.

In an allied field, International Computers Ltd (ICL) is British-based and government-supported and protected in computers: together with other government investment in microprocessors, etc., it could be a revolutionary and British-controlled force affecting all areas of the economy.

Another major area of high technology is aerospace where the scale of investment necessarily goes far beyond private resources and where defence policy is exceptionally important. The existing publicly-owned British Aerospace (threatened by current Tory policies) could, as for instance the union TASS-AUEW has proposed, collaborate more closely with the state-owned Rolls-Royce and British Airways, but also be strengthened by the acquisition of the helicopter, hovercraft and avionics firms in the UK. This would permit planned investment and an integrated approach on buying policies.

In the case of the steel industry, contrary to the approach this book makes, the British Steel Corporation (BSC) under Tory Government pressure is being forcibly contracted, cutting its investment and labour force. The case for integration in the steel industry, capable of meeting all the needs for special steels and tubes, has been long argued and would again allow a coordinated investment programme in a sector absolutely vital for the future of British industry and for meeting the needs of the developing world. That is why the public ownership of, for instance, Tube Investments and Guest Keen and Nettlefolds must be considered.

Finally, given our earlier proposals on North Sea oil and the possible roles of a publicly-owned BP together with the UK operations of Shell, the public ownership of Imperial Chemical Industries (ICI) would provide a dominant force not only in oil but in petrochemicals and other specialist areas of the chemical industry.

These additions to the publicly-owned sector would join the existing nationalized firms and industries. Within the labour movement proposals have been put forward from time to time for extending public ownership to other sectors, such as the entire vehicle industry or the pharmaceutical industry. However, I have tried to avoid being involved in a shopping-list made up of all the proposals made by different groups; they are for discussion. My concern has been to argue for the kind of extensions critically necessary for the AES to be carried forward.

Major financial institutions which channel internal and external flow of funds

Why is it important to the AES to have the greatest possible control of financial flows? In opposition to the report of the Wilson *Committee to Review the Functioning of Financial Institutions*, there is a powerful case for extending public ownership as well as control.

First, the scale of investment needed in all areas of the economy cannot be found from reinvested profits. Because of the 'peculiar' development of British capitalism, large British firms rely on self-financing. But this means that they have to take a very short-run view of what is profitable so as to get their money back quickly. What is desperately needed is long-term investment, at favourable rates of interest, in areas which may also be risky, such as high technology.

The financial institutions, on the other hand, who are the main mobilizers of private funds, invest on a different set of criteria. They prefer government bonds and property to risky ventures in manufacturing and technology. As we shall see, the insurance companies and pension funds have indeed become large-scale owners of company funds, but this is not the same thing as providing funds for large-scale new investment; and they tend to be a cautioning influence on firms rather than an encouraging and innovative one. They desire security as much as they enjoy capital appreciation. The contrast with countries like West Germany and Japan is striking.

We are discussing therefore a positive investment policy pursued by government, involving all sections of business. The argument that what is short is not money but profitable schemes therefore misses the point. With the present system of financing, few schemes could appear profitable.

Second, the concentration of power in the hands of the financial institutions is very substantial; the significance of this is barely understood by the public. Yet these institutions are crucial to government financing and in helping to determine the rate of interest.

They can influence the flow of hot money into or out of the country, helping to precipitate financial crises. They are the largest source of funds in the economy for 'investment', i.e. the acquisition of financial claims, such as bonds or shares. Moreover, what has barely begun to be understood is that non-banking financial companies *now own more than half of the shares of British industrial and commercial companies*. Even more significant, the major buyers of company shares are increasingly the pension funds, including (in the first instance) the pension funds of the public corporations!

These enormous funds are disposed of by a small self-appointed group linked with the City establishment, away from all public discussion and accountability, which – despite innumerable scandals – regulates its own conduct and misconduct. The argument that the financial sector of the economy is already under government control and needs no further control is one that became even more ludicrous when the Tory Government abolished exchange controls. The ability of the banks, for instance, to evade the Government's own objectives, and the beginnings of a large-scale flow of funds overseas, should give rise to some rethinking.

It ought also to be added, when it is argued that the financial institutions are efficient, that a good deal of them are cartelized, with very
limited competition. Moreover, nearly half British families have no
bank accounts compared with more than 90% in France, West
Germany and the US who have; and in the area of insurance, the companies may flourish, but it is less clear that the premium payers receive a
good deal.

For these reasons the position taken by some previous Labour Party
conferences, that public ownership should be extended to (i) the four
private clearing banks which account for most joint-stock banking in
the UK (Barclays, Midland, NatWest and Lloyds); and (ii) the biggest
insurance companies, in particular Prudential, Commercial Union,
Royal, Guardian Royal Exchange, Legal and General, Standard Life,
Norwich Union, should be strongly supported.

This still leaves unanswered the future for pension funds which are
the fastest growing financial institutions, with funds that will make them
the most powerful financial bodies in the land. Amongst the biggest of
them are the funds of existing state-owned enterprises such as the Post
Office, the National Coal Board, British Rail and Electricity Supply, as
well as those of firms like ICI and BP. The pension funds of nationalized
enterprises are now major owners of large private firms!

An obvious and immediate first step is to make such funds more accountable both to the workforce in those enterprises and to the public. A
Labour Party White Paper proposed 50% trade union representation
on pension funds management bodies. A minority report of the Wilson
Committee proposed a national £2 billion lending facility using pension
fund money underwritten by North Sea oil revenues.

Another problem for policy is presented by the building societies.
They have become almost like banks for large numbers of people
(arousing the hostility of the clearing banks); their favoured tax treatment has fostered owner occupation which, in conditions of short
supply, has forced up house prices. As people move, house prices are
refinanced at current market prices, pushing up the amount of credit
needed for further increasing owner occupation. Only a small proportion of the building societies' funds have been available for new building,
and the societies have acted as a cartel on interest rates. Perhaps the
case here is for more cooperation between the building societies, the
government and local authorities in trying to ensure that their funds are
less available for second mortgages and more for new development.

In addition, the Bank of England needs to be made genuinely responsive to national requirements, and Giro expanded and popularized as part of a nationwide integrated banking network.

In this sphere as in others a major and unresolved question is what is to be done about the enormous involvement of all these banks and financial institutions in other countries, including South Africa, Australia, the Far and Middle East, Europe and North America. In developing the AES this will have to be confronted.

Before making an assessment of what these proposals amount to overall, there is the important question of compensation.

How should the present owners be compensated?

Railwaymen, miners, steelworkers and others know what a blight heavy compensation can be on a publicly-owned industry, especially if it needs large-scale investment from borrowed funds. In the past, payment has been in fixed-interest stocks guaranteed by the Treasury and paid as a first charge, whether the industry made profits or not. The fact that inflation has eroded the burden of debt hardly makes it the desired solution.

If we look back at other approaches made by government, these have included basing compensation on the market value of the assets, on net maintainable revenue, and on annual debt charges already incurred.

In general it is right that compensation should be paid, but the special concern should be for individuals rather than companies. There is a widespread feeling that issues of equity are involved, as well as the need for political alliances on which any programme for change must be based. Other approaches that could be considered include, for instance: basing compensation on historical capital costs (what the assets cost when purchased), and not on the stock exchange value (i.e. the current market price of the shares), or on net maintainable values; and giving individuals life annuities. The principle should be accepted that the burden of compensation payments falls on the Treasury and not on the acquired enterprises.

We have now looked at the key areas in which extensions of public ownership has been proposed. What do these amount to in relation to the private sector, and what leverage on it would they provide?

The significance of public ownership proposals

The changes which have so far been proposed should not be

exaggerated or underestimated. Assuming that they took place over a period of time, much of the economy would still remain privately owned and controlled.

At a rough estimate such changes would leave nearly 80% of manufacturing output in private hands, or 70–75% of total industrial output (private ownership would predominate and be complete in the food, drink and tobacco industries; in many sectors of chemical and allied industry; in mechanical engineering; in textiles and the clothing industry; and in building material and miscellaneous manufacturing industries). All foreigner-owned subsidiaries operating in the UK would remain (though American oil companies would lose their ownership stake in North Sea oil).

The commercial and trading sector (including shipping) would be almost entirely in private hands (apart of course from the Co-operative societies).

Farming would remain as it is; so would virtually all firms in building and construction and most existing firms in the private service sector. Most firms in finance and commodity trading would continue, though – as we note below – the banking and insurance area would be profoundly altered.

Some readers will be shocked to find this list so large and extensive (how this private sector should be made publicly accountable is dealt with in the next section); but consider what the public sector would amount to.

First, it would be the major (almost the sole) force in all branches of energy, communications and transport, commanding the infrastructure of the UK.

Second, it would have powerful positions in key investment and high technology as well as other areas, including electrical engineering, electronics and computing, petrochemicals and chemicals, bulk and specialized steels and tubes, and in shipbuilding, vehicles and aerospace.

Third, it would be in direct control of the main central and local banking systems, predominate in insurance, with strong positions in hire purchase and other kinds of credit finance (remembering also that the largest pension funds are those of the public corporations).

Fourth, through its ownership of the largest insurance companies and in association with the pension funds, it would own a large proportion of all company shares.

Fifth, the combined firms and sectors would account for a large share of foreign trade (including invisible earnings) and of all fixed capital investment in the UK.

It is obvious that if to this is added the combined purchasing power of central and local government, powerful instruments for change are available. I am not arguing that every single one of these proposals is crucial or that there are no other additional proposals to be made; only that they represent the kind of massed power needed to go beyond a relatively short-term boost to the economy. Nor am I assuming that these changes can be made overnight; they are bound to be the outcome of a very difficult industrial, social and political struggle.

Again I must underline the point, which cannot be made too often, that none of the advantages come simply from public ownership. State intervention can be disastrous as well as beneficial, despotic as well as democratic. These proposals therefore have to be considered in the context of the entire strategy.

They have not considered the contribution which an extended Cooperative Movement could make, not only in trade where it is already substantial, but in manufacturing, construction and agriculture. It is also here that the local authorities could play a positive and significant role. One obvious and in no sense novel contribution is through the purchase by local authorities of existing factory units and the building of new ones. The new development would be to link the terms for letting these units with agreements on health and safety, trade union recognition, and conditions of employment. A second way is through the encouragement and financial support for cooperative ventures by groups of workers and by existing small businesses.

I have argued that the direction of British society cannot be changed or its problems tackled if it remains dominated by giant, privately controlled firms and financial institutions driven by the aim of private profitability backed by the machinery of state and the government of the day. But a government of the left, with popular support, and powerful leverage of its own (such as that provided by our earlier proposals) must attempt to harness the energy, resources, initiative and self-interest of many sections of employers and management, together with the small and medium firms and the self-employed who would still be crucially important for the fate of the economy.

III HARNESSING AND CONTROLLING THE PRIVATE SECTOR

The attempt to 'gear in' the private sector is itself a major political and

economic requirement for change. It is not only a question of the top
executives and large private shareholders of the giant firms who, with
their international connections, possess great power to support or
sabotage the intentions of a left government. There are the hundreds of
thousands of one-man, small and medium enterprises in manufacturing,
trade and services.

A democratic movement which has majority support needs to be able ∨
to ensure that private capital contributes to the change and does not
sabotage it; and that such a movement not only has power to compel
but can offer support, encouragement and reward. The advantages in
cooperation need to be mutual.

Not surprisingly the issue of accountability and control has arisen
mainly for the small number of large firms, many of them multinational,
who are dominant in most branches of industry, commerce and finance
– perhaps two or three hundred of them.

Here the labour and trade union movement, taking account of international experience, has found a likely instrument: the planning agreement. Tony Benn defined the role of such agreements when he began
work at the Department of Trade and Industry in 1974 (the quotation is
lengthy, but repays careful reading).

The basic objective of the planning agreements system is to secure the confor-
mity of leading companies with national economic priorities, in return for supporting requested industrial developments, giving financial assistance, etc. The
basis for such agreements will therefore include such criteria as price control,
the level of home and overseas sales, the regional distribution of employment,
domestic investment levels, industrial relations practices and product development. These agreements will need to be on a tripartite basis with the unions
involved at the outset. Once corporate policies in these areas had been agreed
on an annual and rolled forward five-year basis, the government would be in a
position to grant selective financial assistance for at least the minimum period
necessary to meet the demands of medium-term corporate planning. Financial
aid to major companies will thus progressively be shifted towards a basis of
support linked to the objectives of the planning agreements. The information
drawn from them will then be available to the Government in planning its own
strategy. The firms to be included in the system will initially number about 100,
controlling about half manufacturing output. Since the great majority of these
100 or so firms have overseas subsidiaries or are themselves part of wider international groupings, this new conditional system of aid, combining both incentives and sanctions, will form an important instrument in securing the com-
pliance of large multinational corporations with the Government's own
economic objectives (Department of Trade and Industry document, 1974).

These ideas not only met with the bitter hostility of the CBI; they were sabotaged by the Labour Government itself; Tony Benn was sacked and removed to the Department of Energy. In the event only two planning agreements (of a sort) were signed – with Chrysler and the National Coal Board.

There are three critical lessons to be learnt from that experience. The first is that planning agreements must be made compulsory. Second, they must be formulated with the active involvement of the workforce and especially of the trade union and shop stewards' movement. This is just as vital for planning agreements with privately owned firms as for public enterprises. It is doubly important when it comes to monitoring the way firms are carrying through their part of the agreement. The efforts made to get firms to disclose their investment, location and employment plans show the need for much stronger powers. Third, planning agreements can only be properly set up within the framework of some overall set of national objectives.

These are the very weaknesses which have limited the effectiveness of the NEDO Sector Working Parties, especially in their relations with the dominant firms.

But if these conditions were established, policies designed to expand the economy would benefit privately-owned firms: there would be growing markets and opportunities for investment, with, where appropriate, substantial financial and other support. Profitability would come from improvements in volume and efficiency, not from profiteering and monopolistic pricing. The large body of managerial and supervisory staff who actually carry out the day-to-day operations of such firms could find satisfaction in a cooperative effort to improve the conditions of the people and the vigour of the economy.

Further advantages could come from the collaboration of public and privately-owned firms both within Britain and across national boundaries (on the European Airbus project for instance).

The problems are real, but so are the possibilities. Firms, even large ones, must not just be seen as single personalities whose entire operations can be determined by a handful of top shareholders and executives. We would expect a powerful democratic movement to have changed the perspectives of many who are in managerial positions; the increased ownership of shares by pension funds and insurance companies are also useful levers. (The fact that most of the largest companies are multinational adds a different dimension – discussed in Section IV below.)

The focus so far has been on the giant firms and the possibility that, through planning agreements with a small number of them, the decisive areas of the economy can be under some kind of coordinated control. What is to be offered the vast numbers of small and middle-sized firms? Their economic role is often underestimated, wrongly. They are very significant in terms of the numbers they employ; in some sectors they are the predominant force; they contribute a great deal of specialization and expertise in a number of spheres. Moreover, in some cities and boroughs, e.g. in parts of London such as Hackney, the public services and local authorities are the largest employers, the rest of the workforce are in small firms. They need reassurance that they have a role to play and that there will be support to help them with their problems. Within the labour movement itself there is much misgiving about this because many small firms offer the most miserable conditions, employ cheap labour, and are hostile to trade union membership.

The line of advance, apart from national provision of funds, will probably lie mainly through the localities and regions. It has been suggested for instance that local authorities could enter into agreements with firms in a locality. The local authorities would provide grants, loans and research facilities to small and medium enterprises and especially encourage consortiums or varying kinds of cooperative arrangements. In return the firms would recognize their social responsibilities in terms of trade union organization, working conditions, release for training and further education, properly-negotiated wage rates and security of employment. Again, this is within a framework of economic growth. It is also possible for local authorities to take a stake in local firms; and to use the influence that comes from being large purchasers of goods and services from local suppliers.

This is one aspect of the AES which has been much neglected but which is vital if popular support is to be won and the strategy successfully pursued.

IV DEALING WITH THE MULTINATIONALS

If there is one development which has altered the way the world capitalist economy has worked since 1945 it is the rise of the multinational companies. Today two-thirds of the trade of the developed world is in the hands of a few hundred multinationals (and half of that is trade between their subsidiaries). Their liquid reserves total perhaps twice the total currency reserves of all the major Central Banks. The largest of them such as Exxon, General Motors, Royal Dutch Shell, have sales revenues greater than the gross national product of half the countries within the OECD (which includes the main capitalist countries of the world).

British capital is second only to the USA in its ownership of capital invested overseas, and in recent years the giant firms and financial institutions have renewed their drive for world expansion. The world activities of the oil companies are well known but in manufacturing, for instance, the fifty largest UK companies now have 36% of their output produced abroad. Not surprisingly, the operations of the multinationals have created deep and world-wide concern. What problems do they raise? One very general way of putting it is that they have outgrown state controls.

Because they plan on a global basis, they can play state against state and worker against worker in terms of how much they invest, in which country or region, in what sector, with what degree of employment, using what technology, and so on. It is relatively simple for them to run down a plant over a considerable time (as Singers did in Clydebank) and then declare it unprofitable and close it down.

They can frustrate the taxation and revenue plans of governments by using various means of shifting income from one country to another through the use of tax havens (like Bermuda) and transfer pricing (where for instance a subsidiary invoices goods to another subsidiary in another country at a low price so as to show a lower profit in the exporting country – useful if the exporting country has higher taxes than the importing one).

They can frustrate the plans of governments to promote exports or reduce imports by their own decisions as to which markets their subsidiaries shall supply (it is well known that the major single importer of foreign cars into the UK has been Fords of UK). They can damage or strengthen a country's currency on the foreign exchange by shifting their vast liquid reserves and by delays in settling accounts.

Moreover, the complex division of labour which the multinationals establish between their subsidiaries, combining specialist production of components in some areas with multi-sourcing and assembly of uniform models in others, makes it difficult for governments and workers to take action against them. In addition, their large resources enable them to use political pressure or sometimes bribery in order to press their interests.

This is certainly a formidable list of problems and it daily becomes more acute. Are governments and people then powerless? At the national level there are two possible lines of action. The first is that some of the multinationals are taken over where the strategy clearly requires it; a number if not all the firms proposed for public ownership in Section II above are multinationals based on the UK (with the exception of Shell which is Anglo-Dutch, though most of its shares are British held). Any proposition to take over all the multinationals operating in the UK is fanciful. But what should be done about the operations of these firms overseas? Are their assets to be disposed of? This is a matter not for gestures but for serious negotiation, the nature of the bargain depending on whether the assets are in a less developed country or in an advanced capitalist economy like the USA.

A second line of action is to try to bring the multinationals within a framework of cooperation so that they can contribute to the overall strategy. The more substantial their operations in Britain, the more reason they have for wanting them to be profitable. The key instrument would obviously be the planning agreement.

In general when we discussed planning agreements the involvement of the workforce to help monitor the progress was stressed; but where firms are heavily involved in foreign operations other instruments are needed. Inland Revenue and Customs, for instance, need special units to deal with possible transfer pricing and unreasonable transfers through royalty and licence payments, control of outward and inward investment, acquisitions abroad, and the use of foreign tax havens.

But we cannot escape the need for international action. Our proposals, however reinforced, cannot deal with the massive problems of control. And there are additional complications. Other countries may not accept the right of a British government to impose constraint on British-owned subsidiaries operating within those countries, any more than we want American law used to dictate what Fords or Vauxhalls do in the UK. Companies as well as governments can take advantage of this, as when subsidiaries of BP and Shell 'busted' sanctions against Rhodesia. There is a continuing struggle to compel international organizations and the governments which belong to them to agree on codes of conduct to be enforced on the behaviour of the multinationals. Not surprisingly the greatest pressure has come from the less-developed countries who have suffered most, but increasing pressure comes from the international labour movement. Such codes of conduct have been drawn up by the United Nations, the OECD, the EEC and the ILO; but what is needed are codes that are *enforceable*. In such codes the following key areas would have to be covered: public accountability; disclosure of information; social obligations of companies; control of direct foreign investment and takeovers; restrictive business practices and pricing; taxation; transfers of technology and role of the multinationals in the developing countries; short-term capital movements. There are obviously conflicts of national interest when governments compete for the favour of multinational investment, but at the same time even right-wing circles are worried. The movement for such enforeable codes is growing.

Perhaps the most important foundation for international action even at government level is the strengthening of cooperation and solidarity between the workers of different countries, especially where they work for a given firm.

The most urgent thing is for action now without waiting for some change in government which can build up the support of public opinion here and abroad. The 'internationalization' of capital continues apace. The longer the delay in controlling it, the more difficult such control becomes. This is a world-wide democratic issue, critical for any kind of democratic control of the national economy.

V THE MECHANISMS OF INVOLVEMENT AND PLANNING

The left in Britain has been very fond of talking about planning but has done surprisingly little work on it. There are honourable exceptions ranging, over the post-war period, from G. D. H. Cole to Stuart Holland. In this brief section, continuing the discussion in Section I, I have drawn on the work of individuais and party programmes such as those issued by the Labour Party and the Communist Party. The suggestions I make are not intended as a kind of 'optimal' structure but only to stimulate further thought. They are concerned not with democratic planning in some future completely transformed British society but with proposals which have their roots in the situation we are in. Several times in Section I, the phrase 'the democratic process' was used. What does it mean?

Essentially, it means a *movement* which involves the widest circles of people in discussion and action on all matters which affect them. It is a movement which has to use existing representative institutions built up over long periods of time, which are regarded as 'legitimate' in the sense that they are elected bodies who are authorized to make decisions: the obvious examples are the House of Commons and the local authorities.

The political activity of parties is expressed in these bodies. That aspect of the democratic process is very partial, we know: there remain an unelected and obstructive House of Lords which should be abolished, and a mass of traditional House of Commons procedure which serves to delay and obstruct.

Nevertheless, any planning system must take its authority from the elected representatives and the government which is formed on that basis. Its *real* authority of course rests on the popular support for what it does. In terms of formal structure, there could be a Cabinet Committee or even Department of Planning (which should itself have a representative character as well as being serviced by experts), and a system of reporting to a House of Commons Committee (for which the precedents are now well established).

However, before anything more is said about machinery, the discussion on 'the democratic process' needs to be taken further. Our society is composed of conflicting classes and of bargaining and interest groups. The organizations of these classes and groups (such as the CBI, the employers' federations, the TUC) are engaged in continuous bargaining and decision-making which go on behind the back of parliament and can hardly be monitored by parliament even if it wishes; indeed parliament cannot review the bulk of activity of the departments of government itself.

The extension of the activities of the state centrally, and especially the work of local authorities, means that they pervade every aspect of life from the cradle to the grave. In that sense, the institutions and machinery, the entire network of bodies and committees involving the health, education, other welfare services, local government committees, etc., become themselves areas of contest over policies and directions. And these touch the lives of everyone.

When we talk about democratic control it would be totally unreal to confine it to parliamentary control. Political parties cannot capture all the interests, desires and possibilities especially at the grass roots' level. The democratic process must also therefore include the fostering of every kind of community organization. The growth of the women's movement and the degree to which its concerns are widely discussed and taken up is vital to any serious extension of democracy.

Nevertheless, no society can function if it is in a continuous state of paralysis or endless discussion where no decisions can be taken. In that sense bodies set up as representative of the electorate, such as the House of Commons and local authorities, have crucial responsibilities. But the only guarantee that the activities of such bodies have social approval is the continuous movement and pressure from those who feel directly the impact of every change and each decision.

In terms of planning mechanisms this suggests, as a possible structure for an initial period, a Department of Planning as part of the government, responsible to a special parliamentary committee. Together with government departments these bodies between them would have the responsibility for formulating economic policies outlining a number of different approaches. Experience of planned economies has shown that, if people are to be brought into genuine debate and consultation, they must have the chance to consider a number of different 'scenarios' as well as to add to them.

The broadly-agreed approach would become the framework for the planning agreements with the one or two hundred largest firms, and these firms in turn would be grouped around the most appropriate government departments, assuming for the moment that departments such as Energy, Industry, Environment, Food and Fisheries continue in some form or another. The advantages are: the existence of a democratically-agreed perspective backed by resources and with popular support. Within the largest firms, the planning agreements would have been worked out with the active involvement of the workforce, the shop stewards and the unions. The government departments together with the enterprises have the advantage of being familiar with the changing technology and market conditions which the firms face, not only within the UK but overseas. Without the flexibility which such knowledge alone can provide, the agreements themselves would be worthless or positively damaging.

There is in addition the regional or local aspect (and a national aspect if we consider the likelihood that Scottish and Welsh Assemblies would at some stage come into being). The activity of political parties, trade unions, community groups, and ad hoc pressure organizations, together with local authorities, could make such regional/national planning bodies much more responsive to grass roots' opinion and needs.

As the counter-attack against Tory policies develops, a much wider and constructive discussion must take place on how democratic control of the national economy is to be established. No special virtues are claimed for the suggestions made above.

Do we need a National Enterprise Board?

The idea of a National Investment Board or National Enterprise Board (NEB) has been around in the labour movement for decades. Towards the end of the sixties the left in the Labour Party conceived of the NEB as taking a controlling stake in about 25 of the top hundred manufacturing companies, together with the holdings already held by the state. The NEB was to become a major force in industrial investment, financed partly out of profits and partly from large-scale government funds. This proposal was, as we know, undermined by the Labour Government when the NEB became in fact a kind of merchant bank, but with a higher proportion of 'lame ducks' under its wing; and this was itself further watered down by the 1979 Tory Government.

But is the NEB even in its 'strong' version a good method? Of course the demand for large-scale government supported investment has already been argued for in our earlier chapters; and in so far as the Labour Party, the TUC, and other bodies propose these funds to be channelled through a strengthened NEB, it should be supported. Nevertheless, there is no value in having a vast conglomerate organization separated from the rest of the public sector (which would itself be enlarged, e.g. through public ownership of financial institutions) as a useful planning instrument. In so far as the NEB derived some of its inspiration from the experience of the IRI in Italy, we must also acknowledge the dangers of empire building, involving further layers of bureaucracy and gigantism which are also part of its experience.*

The idea of an NEB cuts across the need to plan on a sectoral basis across the economy. BP for instance, together with BNOC (in whatever structure was created) could best be part of an energy sector linked with the Ministry of Energy than a (rather overwhelming) part of an already vast NEB. In principle, that would be true also of British Leyland. None of this is meant in any dogmatic sense. It is obvious enough that those who believe democratic planning is necessary have also to open out the discussion as to its forms. We are left with one major dimension not so far discussed: democracy within the plant and the enterprise.

VI   INDUSTRIAL DEMOCRACY

Not a single resolution on this issue appeared at the 1980 TUC. Yet,

* The Istituto per la Ricostruzione Industriale (IRI) came into existence in the thirties and expanded into an enormous holding company in post-war Italy.

introducing a pamphlet on industrial democracy, Moss Evans, General Secretary of the Transport and General Workers Union, wrote:

In a democratic society, democracy does not stop short at the factory gate or the office door. We spend a large part of our lives at work and invest our skills and energies in industry. The pioneers of our union and of the labour movement fought long and hard to win a vote for working people in parliamentary elections. There is now a growing realization that our democracy needs extending. It must enable those who work in industry to participate in the decisions made there, which can vitally affect their working lives (*Industrial Democracy*, TGWU pamphlet, 1978).

This was written in 1978. How little say workers have in the enterprises in which they work, whether public or private, has been brutally driven home by the closures and redundancies announced daily now over many months.

The discussion on industrial democracy may seem very remote in this harsh climate, but the need for those who work in public and private enterprises to intervene in the decisions being taken, to insist on different ones and to have advance knowledge of plans which affect them in any important way, has become *more* important, not less. An alternative economic strategy must have built into it an increase in democratic control at the level of the enterprise and the plant. The right to work and the extension of democracy to the workplace are ideas under attack, and the labour movement (and for that matter, all democrats) have suffered defeats. It is understandable that the need to mobilize all the available strength to defend the trade unions themselves and their ability to bargain becomes a priority. But attack is the best defence, and that means a struggle to push forward the areas of collective bargaining, and to intensify the demand for information and disclosure on firms' plans. The foundation for any change is persistent and determined activity by the trade union and shop-stewards' movement, involving and responding to the membership. But in this field, as in all others, advance can only come if credible policies are put forward and if the labour and trade union movement is seen as extending democratic rights in every area.

The appeal to many people of the alternative plans put forward, for instance, by Lucas Aerospace, is that they offer a possible perspective or organizing production on different principles and of involving all the people who are the creative forces whether manual, managerial and technical. We shall discuss the significance of some of these alternative plans in the last chapter.

At this point we want to put forward a few proposals that need to be part of an alternative strategy. In doing so, we must distinguish between publicly-owned industries and those which remain in private hands. We are involved in a struggle to make the nationalized industries part of a system of democratic control; *our proposals for extending public ownership have meaning within an alternative strategy only if large measures of industrial democracy are built into them.* The private sector on the other hand has as its primary aim profitable accumulation.

In the case of planning agreements for instance, this difference must affect the way the workforce takes part in either preparing or supporting them; though in both public and private enterprises the trade unions and shop stewards must avoid confusing their role as negotiators, based on the independence of the trade union movement, with that of workforce representatives concerned with enterprise planning. In *publicly-owned industries* (as proposed by the Communist party) we could envisage a single management board for each enterprise accountable to the workforce and to parliament (representing the community at large). This board should have a *majority* of elected workers and trade union representatives from inside and outside the industry. In addition it would contain government-appointed representatives who must be committed to building up a publicly-owned and democratically-controlled enterprise; and there should also be representatives of the community (such as local authorities, community bodies and consumer groups). Trade union officers and stewards who are involved in negotiating wages and conditions must naturally not be the same as those who are workers and trade union representatives on the board.*

The question of worker-directors *in private firms* is far more difficult, because there is a real danger of workforce representatives becoming absorbed in the higher management 'ethos', opening up divisions between workers and offering possibilities of corruption. These dangers are not confined to the private sector; nevertheless they are greater in privately-owned firms because of their privacy, commercial secrecy and reduced public accountability. The most powerful instruments here must be the bargaining strength of the workforce itself through its trade

---

* At plant level there could be either a works' council separate from the shop stewards' committee, or a shop stewards' committee with mandatory and consultative powers, including powers of veto on management appointments.

union and shop steward organization, insisting on intervening in managerial decisions. In the large firms, if planning agreements become compulsory – as we propose – the key decisions finally arrived at between the company and the planning commission (or appropriate government department) would necessarily involve the agreement of the workers themselves and their organization.

So far we have talked as if everyone worked in industrial enterprises whether public or private. But millions work in the public services (in health, education, welfare, etc.) and in local authorities. The issue of democratic control is no less real there, but it becomes much clearer in such areas that there are *two* aspects to such democratic control. The first is the accountability of these services to the people they serve, i.e. to the local communities. Extending democracy means involving the community far more, and more deeply. The second aspect is of course to allow those who work in these services to have a say in the way they function. In local authorities for instance, it has been suggested that representatives of the workforce should have a place on council committees with the right to speak and vote on them.

Although community involvement seems more obvious in the case of services, it is in practice no less valid for industry. That is why, in any proposals for a system of democratic planning, the involvement of people at local, regional and 'interest group' level is important.

I am not going to try to summarize a chapter which has covered so much ground. The underlying argument is that we cannot get sustained economic growth in the interests of the people and under their control without changes in the social and property relationships involving a major shift of power from big business to the people. I have tried to outline what those changes might be as a basis for further discussion. But democratic control of the national economy means that Britain must be able to regulate its relationships with the rest of the world economy in a way which is mutually profitable, which leads us to the major question of foreign trade.

6 Britain, Foreign Trade and the Import Problem

An alternative economic strategy must have a new foreign trade strategy or else it will collapse.

In recent years, whether the economy has been growing or not, a rising tide of imports has taken a higher proportion of the home market; industries and sectors of industries have been threatened with contraction or shut down. Since 1970 more than 1 million jobs have been lost in manufacturing. Between 1977 and 1979 alone the volume of exports rose by 3% while the volume of imports rose by 30%.

The slow-down in the growth of world trade in the seventies is part of the new era in which we live. As a result, competitive pressures have increased and rivalry between states and capitalist groupings has become sharper. Accusations and counter-accusations of dumping are made each day; trade has become increasingly managed by governments, directly or indirectly, openly or covertly, and even by international groupings like the EEC. In 1974, 36% of all OECD trade was managed, in the sense that it was controlled in some way (apart from tariffs), and 4% in the case of manufacturing. By 1979 these figures had risen to 42% and 13% respectively. In addition, a large amount of trade is controlled by a small number of multinationals.

It is hardly surprising that import controls have become a major political issue, not only in the UK but worldwide. In one sense it is a symptom of a problem which everyone must face who is concerned with an alternative strategy: should the prospects for the UK economy be determined by the rivalry of capitalist groupings, or should we try to shape our trading relations according to the broad objectives we set for British society? In that sense, the term *import controls* is inadequate; the issue is wider than that. The *planned growth of foreign trade* expresses our aim less defensively.

The growing impact of capitalist recession on British industry has forced Britain to confront the major change which has taken place in its world position. The order that prevailed under US leadership from the late forties until the beginning of the seventies has been breaking down. No one can go back; a different order is being constructed. But in whose interests?

Any notion that we can opt out of the world economy is simply ludicrous; we are deeply embedded in a trading and financial network which cannot be discarded by Act of Parliament. That pattern is the result of the entire history of British capitalism. Powerful vested interests are built into our exporting and importing networks and into the financial services centred on the City of London.

One third of all Britain's goods and services and one quarter of our manufactured output are exported; one half of our food is imported; over a quarter of all the manufactured goods we consume is imported. This is apart from the vast quantity of essential raw and basic materials needed for our economy to function. In terms of the actual goods we buy and sell, the earnings with which we buy the raw materials and foodstuffs have in the past depended heavily on Britain exporting more manufactured goods than it bought. Here there has been a massive sea-change. That surplus is disappearing. Between 1970 and 1979 our exports of manufactures rose by one half and the share of exports in our manufacturing has continued to fall; our imports of manufactures rose two-and-a-half times and import penetration continued to rise. Even in the case of the amount of the services we sell abroad, the signs of stagnation are plain.

In one sense the danger has been 'masked' by North Sea oil; we have become almost self-sufficient so we are no longer importing large quantities of foreign oil. But in another sense oil has been used to help push the exchange value of the pound above what it would otherwise be and, together with high interest rates, has made our exports less competitive and imports more competitive. That is a theme we shall come back to. We cannot opt out of the world economy, but do we need to take the pattern of foreign trade we have for granted? We know why business interests want foreign trade and freedom to move their capital around. But what do the *people* of Britain want foreign trade to do?

First, to finance the needs of a growing economy for the food-stuffs and basic materials needed and that we ourselves do not produce; to finance the semi-manufactures and capital goods and the licences which will advance our technology (which we now need to import in quantity — so much has our position changed); and to finance the consumer goods which increase the well-being of consumers and their freedom of choice.

Second, to provide jobs and increase employment in industries and services which have been or could be built up to serve markets abroad. Third, to contribute to the development and industrialization of the less-developed countries. This is a *moral* duty; at the same time it can provide expanding markets for UK industry and secure necessary imports.

These three reasons explain why the people's interests require efficient industries and services which can provide what others want, and why international cooperation and stable world monetary arrangements involving the third world and socialist countries, as well as the advanced capitalist countries, are needed. We can and need to take advantage of specializations and the division of labour on a world scale, but what is *not* in the popular interests is for our economy to be at the mercy of trade and financial decisions taken by giant industrial and financial multinationals and by blocs of rival capitalist groups whether organized in the EEC or by the IMF, dominated by the Group of Ten.

The policies followed by the Tory Government have been inflicting great damage; the Tories have, as we discussed in earlier chapters, attempted to carry through a severe credit squeeze in which high interest rates become an instrument to contract demand and so bring down the rate of inflation. Then, they argue, interest rates can come down. But high interest rates have brought into Britain enormous flows of hot money which in turn has kept the pound riding high in world money markets. This, as everyone knows, penalizes exports and rewards imports. In addition, North Sea oil itself makes overseas investors fond of sterling; together with high interest rates, Britain has offered an irresistible combination. So we have had the spectacle of a super-charged currency and an industry being driven into the ground.

Because North Sea oil is expected to produce an overall surplus in Britain's balance of payments, which would itself keep the exchange rate of the pound high, leading bankers and financiers argued the case for using the gains from North Sea oil to invest overseas on a large scale.

The support of the Tory Government for such a policy led it to abolish all exchange controls. But its actions have set up severe contradictions. Abolishing exchange controls, which was one objective, has made it harder for the Government to control the money supply which it said was its central objective. In addition, though investment abroad has increased, the financial institutions still prefer the UK for the moment as long as interest rates in Britain are higher than those overseas.

This combination of a high exchange rate and high interest rates has severely hit manufacturing industry in Britain. But 'rebel' Tory supporters, like Sir Fred Catherwood, propose as their solution that Britain should join the European Monetary System, which in effect means linking the exchange rate of the pound to the German mark, tying it to our main rivals in Western Europe. An exchange rate fixed in that way would weaken the ability of Britain to decide its *own* economic policy.

What kind of foreign economic strategy is needed?

This is bound to be amongst the trickiest of all problems because it is only partly under the control of British governments; we are involved with many others in our industrial, commercial and financial transactions. Yet an alternative economic strategy will collapse if the foreign trade problems are unresolved.

On past experience, if we expand the economy an even faster growth will take place in imports of basic materials, food, semi-manufactures and consumer goods. The consequences are that such a rise, if large enough, will outstrip our ability to finance it. There would be a crisis of confidence in sterling and it would depreciate. Import prices would rise, real wages fall; we would be back with 'stop-go'. In addition, the fact that the increased spending power based on higher government spending has been 'dissipated' on imports would stop the 'reflation' of the economy from getting under way.

A share of rising imports on British markets has powerful effects which are multiplied as they move through the economy. If imports rise as a share in domestic sales, it follows that the demand for what we produce ourselves falls correspondingly; that reduces the incomes from those engaged in producing in Britain and this in turn reduces both consumption and investment. A vicious circle sets in which leads to fewer people being employed, less investment, lower efficiency, less capacity; and so the resistance to further import penetration weakens.

If our exports could expand sufficiently the problem would not be so acute; but what has been happening is that when incomes in Britain rise by 1%, our demand for imports rises by *more than* 1%; when the income of the rest of the world rises by 1%, its demand for Britain's exports rises by *less than* 1%. We need to know why if we are to know what to do about it.

It could be because our exports are too highly priced. If that were so, then devaluing the pound would solve the problem. It is true that by the summer of 1980 the pound was damagingly high, and some devaluation would help, but it is not the most effective answer, at least in the longer term. This is because the most important cause over the long period has not been price; even when the price competitiveness of British exports has been maintained, their share of the world total continued to fall. This suggests that the UK is not producing what is wanted in type, design and quality. If *that* is the case, devaluation is only a temporary relief, and investment, modernization and increasing innovation in British industry and especially in manufacturing are vital.

We are back again at the investment proposals in Chapter 4. Why are we putting this stress on manufacturing? Not because of some fetish with material products, but because manufacturing exports have to provide us with the greater part of our foreign earnings so as to finance the imports we need (services cannot do that, as we have shown). Manufacturing industry is necessary to provide work and use the skills we have of a large part of the economy and of the labour force. This is especially true of a number of regions such as Scotland and the North West. Manufacturing industry, especially investment goods in high technology areas, is also crucial to increasing industrial efficiency and providing the resources for expanding the service sector; it is therefore vital for the overall balance and integration of the economy.

The fact has to be faced that if British manufacturing is inefficient, and its products not what customers abroad want, our exports will not prosper and our ability to finance the expansion of the economy must suffer. Without such changes, no foreign trade or exchange rate policy can do much in the long run.

But such changes do take time. Even at this moment, we cannot and should not allow industries to collapse; that is why the demand for *emergency selective import controls* to protect textiles, clothing, vehicles and other sectors, has become so widespread. It has been pressed with growing urgency by workers and unions in the industries affected. Many firms are under threat and have taken part in joint pressure on the Tory Government. Some Tory MPs have taken up the call. Essentially it is a demand to extend the protection which already exists even in Britain. The campaign for such emergency controls must be broadened out into a much wider demand without which the AES would become a dead duck — for the *planned growth of foreign trade.*

The planned growth of foreign trade

Strategic control (rather than emergency selective controls) is necessary to allow the economy to grow without the dangers engendered earlier. A growing economy must mean the growth of imports; the point is to ensure that such growth is geared into the even faster growth of our own industry, and that imports help that to happen. That is certain to mean changes in the composition of imports. What is the point of using vast amounts of foreign currency for the unrestricted import of foreign built cars (even by the overseas subsidiaries of multinational companies operating in Britain – Fords for instance), when we are perfectly capable of producing cars in Britain, providing more jobs and income for people in Britain? The foreign currency available might be better spent on fewer foreign cars, and on more technology. Section II below deals with the arguments and counterarguments of such controls.

How is control of imports to be exercised?

At the risk of offending the 'purists', there are three main instruments to consider. One is to make imports dearer by putting on a *tariff* (Blake and Ormerod, 1980, for instance, propose a 10% tariff on manufactured and semi-manufactured goods over the next four years). The second is to devalue the pound which makes all imports dearer in terms of sterling and all exports cheaper if exporters take advantage of it to cut export prices. That is the view pressed, especially by the National Institute of Economic Review, among others. The third way is by more direct control of either or both the volume and value of imports through quotas and licences, and is clearly related to planning agreements, and government and local authority purchasing policies. It is worth saying a bit more about each.

First, raising tariffs on manufactures and semi-manufactures is a way of discouraging imports because their prices will be pushed up relative to domestic prices by the amount of the tariff (10% or whatever). The income from tariffs would be available for subsidies and for tax reductions so that the overall tax burden would not rise.

The second method, devaluation, is the one which is often debated as the best alternative to raising tariffs or use of quotas. In effect, devaluation increases the prices of *all* imports (subject to the qualifications suggested earlier); it cannot be selective. And it acts as a subsidy to exporters by allowing them to sell more cheaply abroad and/or take a bigger profit on their exports.

As things stood in the autumn of 1980 some devaluation would have helped to cut imports and encourage exports. But here again there are serious problems especially in the longer run, because (*a*) getting the right amount of devaluation and keeping it in some appropriate range is not easy because that also depends on what other countries do; (*b*) it is slow to work; (*c*) it increases the cost of living and reduces real wages; if workers resist this by winning increased money wages then the 'benefit' of devaluation will be lost; (*d*) and finally, there are reasons to believe that it will not be used by many firms to cheapen exports but to increase profits. Since much of our foreign trade is in the hands of multinationals who also import/export between their subsidiaries they will not be keen to let devaluation alter their market strategies.

Devaluation therefore is limited as an instrument of strategic planning of foreign trade. This brings us to our third group.

The third group of instruments are designed to be much more precise in controlling the volume and value of imports, and they can be applied in a way which discriminates by products. These methods are by physical quotas (so many tons of this or that; so many machines, etc.) or by value. In the latter case one procedure could be that the government calculates the foreign currency available after meeting essential needs, and auctions import licences to that amount. Without exchange controls it would be impossible to make use of quota licences, because these are 'entitlements' to amounts of foreign currency for financing imports. This latter method makes use of the market mechanism. Such methods do not raise import prices, so they do not in themselves threaten to raise the cost of living.

But the strategic approach to trade needs to be looked at in a much broader way.

In Chapters 4 and 5 we looked at a government-initiated large-scale investment programme linked with planning agreements between government and the largest public and private firms. What this means is that a major effort is made to revitalize and strengthen the productive power of British industry and at the same time ensure that the export and importing strategies fit into the overall objectives. Central government, local authorities, and the major publicly-owned and private firms and financial institutions between them account for the greater part of all exports and imports both of goods and services, as well as the major part of all domestic investment and a very large part of all demand for UK goods and services. Their buying policies alone can exercise great influence.

These proposals in combination not only offer the possibilities of planned growth of imports but tackle the deeper and long-run problem of making sure that our economy can grow and that we can export to meet the objectives of economic and social advance.

Perhaps this will make it clearer why the growing demand for selective and emergency import controls must be broadened out into a much wider campaign. If this fails to happen and other measures are not taken, then other problems will arise. Left by itself it can be a purely defensive measure which will do little for the long-run development of the economy or the industry; it can arouse strong consumer resistance because consumers will be paying higher prices than they have been before protection; in the absence of other gains from this there will be room for division and conflict. There are many employers and Tories who support such emergency controls; their use is already extending and may go a good deal further even under a Tory government. But its direction will most likely be against the third world and not, for instance, against the USA and West Germany, or against the practices of the multinationals.

Overseas investment policy and foreign exchange control

The greater part of this chapter has been concerned with trade and especially the problem of planned control of imports. But, as already argued, an alternative economic strategy is not viable without a comprehensive foreign economic policy. I do not claim that this chapter presents this, but a mention, however brief, must be made of overseas investment policy and control of foreign exchange. The need for controls on flows of capital has been well understood by governments of all kinds. They are needed now and must be part of any demands being made now; they would be vital for any government intending to implement the AES.

Exchange control is needed because 'hot money' moves fast and a left government would certainly meet a 'flight from sterling' (which would start even in the expectation of such a government). But in any case, large movements of funds across national boundaries can be highly destabilizing. However, perhaps an even larger policy issue concerns the import and export of capital in the sense of long-term capital as against short-term funds (or 'hot money').

As we saw above, British capital is the second largest foreign investor in the world. If anything, the scale of its investment overseas has been increasing in the last decade, especially into Western Europe and North America. The bulk of that direct investment has come mainly out of reinvested profits earned overseas, and by borrowing outside the UK. That is beginning to change since the Tory Government abolished all exchange controls.

Here again, because most foreign investment is carried out by a small number of very large firms, the question of planning agreements becomes part of an alternative approach. Our main concern would be to ensure that investment is used to strengthen British industry; we would be wary of plans to build up new capacity overseas in developed countries which compete with us. In contrast, we would see investment in the less-developed countries as part of a series of planned trading agreements. We would wish to make the foreign balance less dependent on receiving interest and dividends from overseas investment. Planning agreements should negotiate the extent to which profits are brought back into the UK or exported from the UK. But that will leave many thorny questions for negotiation, not only with firms but between governments who will be affected by the decisions taken here.

There is also the question of foreign investment in Britain. Quite apart from wanting the existing operations in Britain to succeed, we would be interested in importing skill and techology. By strengthening democratic control the AES would make the economy less vulnerable to foreign investment and better able to use it where needed. The major exception is in the case of foreign ownership of North Sea oil. The public ownership of North Sea oil will mean, apart from payments made under service contracts to any foreign firms that are needed, a check to the growing flow of profit from Britain mainly to the United States.

Rising import penetration has led to a widespread public debate, a discussion that needs, as I have argued, to be extended and broadened. There are practical, theoretical, economic and political objections to the proposals we have made. Three of these are dealt with in Section II below, but the reader must keep in mind that the argument of this book is for the strategic, planned control of foreign trade in an expanding economy. Some objectors do not distinguish this from selective emergency import controls.

II THREE OBJECTIONS ANSWERED

First objection: 'Import controls are chauvinist measures, exporting unemployment to the workers of other countries especially of the Third World.'

It is true that emergency import controls can have that effect; the argument for *strategic* import controls is that they would allow the British economy to grow and imports would also grow. What has to be controlled is their rate of growth and their composition. The question is usually asked by those who say they believe in planning; so what objection can there to to planned foreign trade?

Of course, in principle, anything that happens in an economy involved in foreign trade will have effects on other trading partners and the workers in them. For instance, increasing efficiency in producing exports will have effects on workers who work in rival export industries. What has the most devastating effects of all on workers everywhere are deflationary restrictive economic policies designed to increase the reserve army of labour. To break out of such policies requires planned foreign trade; to isolate import controls as a chauvinist measure is simple-minded.

Is the objection, however, meant to suggest that the labour and trade union movement can somehow ignore such matters as subsidies by foreign governments to their exporting industries, the balance of payments, and the problems of foreign debt and control? This is clearly absurd. The British people must concern themselves with the people of other countries; we live in an interdependent world. But what the AES *cannot* do is solve the internal class problems of other countries; and what happens in Britain should not be determined by the policies of, for instance, an aggressive capitalist class in Japan, Brazil or Taiwan. Conflicts of interest do exist and cannot be wished away; perhaps in some future world socialist scheme these would all be avoided, but we cannot act now on that basis.

Nevertheless, the demand for immediate protection is often accompanied by deep resentment and hostility against, e.g., 'cheap labour' abroad. To imagine that Britain's problems would be solved in this way and not by changes in the social system is mistaken.

It is widely put about that the exports of manufactures from the third world are the greatest danger to British industry. This is not true. In nearly every sector (including textiles) the main import threat for the UK comes from other developed countries, particularly from Japan, the United States and West Germany. In 1975 only 18% of our textile imports came from the developing countries. We import 10% of our manufactured imports from the third world, but it buys 28% of our exports and we have a surplus on trade in manufactured goods with it of £6 million. The enlargement of the EEC by the addition of Spain, Greece and Portugal will lead to still further handicaps for third world exports. However, this does not mean no problems exist for the UK. A group of rapidly industrializing third world countries (Hong Kong, Singapore, South Korea and Taiwan) accounts for one half the third world's manufacturing exports. We do not need to underwrite the 'forced' exporting industries of those countries, reinforced by their own big business and the major multinational and financial groups of advanced capitalism. But we are deeply concerned with the economic development of less-developed countries, whose industrialization can be damaged by protectionist policies.

What is most needed is a positive programme of trade on a long-term planned basis between Britain and third world countries which will help them to develop their economies and domestic markets. It is the expansion of the domestic economies of the advanced countries which led to trade in manufactures between them becoming the major source of growth in world trade in the post-war world. If such plans could be carried through with the third world on a long-term basis, major new markets for machines and every kind of capital equipment would be created.

A number of third world countries are certainly becoming major forces in some labour intensive industries (though their advance will certainly not remain in those sectors only); the advanced countries will increasingly move into further and new areas of high technology. Whilst there should be no automatic assumption that labour-intensive industries as such have no future in the UK, the significance of the AES is that it would permit the structural changes to take place in a planned way, offering the greatest mutual benefit.

Second objection: 'Protection will raise domestic price and wages, and will featherbed inefficient industries and hold back innovation.'

We need to spell out the objection more fully. Prices will rise, it is argued, (*a*) because there will be more demand for UK products and that will push up prices, and (*b*) because tariffs and/or devaluation will increase the price of imports which will get passed on to the consumer. The featherbedding, of course, will arise because there will be less competition and so less incentive to improve. Emergency import controls are obviously more vulnerable to this objection. But what about strategic controls? To deal with prices first. In general, research shows that prices change with changes in costs and not so much with changes in demand; if demand rises, it is output (not prices) that will rise, just as, if demand falls, it is output (not prices) which tends to be cut. Strategic controls as part of the AES should therefore boost output and have a limited effect on prices. In addition output tends to encourage improvements in productivity and rising productivity can hold back price increases by reducing unit costs. For that reason also, the investment and modernization plans become important in the longer run. Price control would also be available to prevent profiteering.

Those who wish to use tariffs propose to exempt foodstuffs and raw materials. In the case of semi- and finished manufactures the tax revenue from tariffs could be used to reduce VAT, for instance, and so keep the general price level constant. Devaluation on the other hand would increase domestic prices, worsen the terms of trade and cut real wages unless money wages rise; that is why its use has to be as limited as possible. The use of quotas and licences need not have these negative effects. However, the main argument remains that strategic controls will enable the domestic economy to expand; the result will be that real incomes will rise, so will tax revenues, and tax *cuts* may be necessary.

The danger of featherbedding is real, especially if emergency import controls are used in isolation. Competition can in certain circumstances be a very useful incentive.

The problem can be tackled in different ways but the first point to make is that economic stagnation, even without protection, has proved to have the most damaging effect on investment efficiency and productivity. That is why when it comes to support for industries in difficulty, and the cost of state support, we must look at the *social* costs of unemployment and the *social* benefits of keeping people at work even in inefficient plants.

Second, domestic firms can and do compete with each other. There are some fields where that competition is wasteful but others where it is useful. There is room for a competitive policy, something we have so far not discussed.

Emergency controls for industries in difficulty may well mean maintaining higher prices than would prevail with uncontrolled imports; and if that were the main plank of an alternative economic strategy, criticism and discontent amongst consumers would certainly build up. Such protection is necessary as an immediate relief but, without the rest of the strategy, the cost of living would rise. But even so, some estimates suggest that the gain to the general welfare would be immensely greater with total production of goods and services 20% higher.

Third objection: 'Protection will bring the strong likelihood of retaliation and we will be worse off than before.'

This is an objection strongly held (or used) by opponents of strategic import controls, and it worries many supporters of such controls. Countries can pursue 'beggar my neighbour' policies which will leave everyone worse off; not *every* country can have a surplus in its trade balance at the same time. Nevertheless, if we look at the problem in terms of *economics*, the danger of retaliation has been exaggerated. Why?

First: since we are considering strategic import controls, i.e. controls designed to let the domestic economy expand with controlled *growth* of imports, there is no case or cause for retaliation in terms of the UK as a market. It will be (and is) far worse for those who export to us if our economy declines and deflation reigns.

Second: suppliers of raw materials and foodstuffs will greatly benefit by UK expansion since we will need much greater amounts.

Third: broadly, if the AES works, the longer-run outcome would be continued growth in imports of semi-manufactures and even manufactured goods. But it is still possible that certain categories of imported finished manufactures would grow at a much slower rate or even show some fall. No doubt these exporters would feel aggrieved. But what would be the basis for retaliation? The countries which would be affected, like Japan, West Germany, and North America, already sell much more to us than we do to them. Disrupting trade by retaliating would hurt them more than it hurts us. Their best hope in fact – again in economic terms – would be for our strategy to succeed in boosting the British economy. Even if some measure of retaliation were carried out be some countries, the UK would be in a stronger position to survive. One result of North Sea oil is that the pound is less open to attack than it would otherwise be and the substantial reserves and oil revenues are powerful supports.

Fourth: even countries that might consider retaliation have to take into account that they are themselves practising very considerable measures of protection. Some of these arguments apply also to emergency protective controls as *all* governments come under pressure.

For all the reasons given, judged on economic grounds, the fear of retaliation looks much less serious than at first sight. But that does not dispose of the problem, because any government seriously attempting to carry through the AES *as a package* would be seen as challenging the entire system of big business. It would inevitably be associated with other broad changes in foreign and international policy. The danger is that international business and foreign governments would try to use all the weapons at its disposal to create an unmanageable crisis. That is a much broader issue to which we return in the final chapter.

It is obviously far better for a government pursuing the AES to do so with as much agreement with its trading partners as possible. In the long run international organizations like the IMF, in which the US has the power of veto, need major reforms which would also allow them to accommodate planned economies, represent the less-developed countries, and have more democratic constitutions. If that is not possible, new international bodies would need to be established.

7 The Common Market – Who Wants It?

The British people do not need the EEC; more specifically, they need to get out. This is the more necessary as the struggle for a new direction in economic policy gains ground. In 1975, by a two to one majority (of the 64% who voted), after a massive and powerfully financed campaign in favour of membership, Britain chose to stay in the Community.

In April 1980 a poll financed by the EEC itself showed that in Britain just about half of those interviewed were against membership and less than a quarter believed there were advantages in staying in. In a survey of members published in August 1980 the Institute of Directors revealed that half those interviewed did not think British membership on present terms was beneficial and 73% said they had gained nothing from the EEC. A survey of active Tory constituency workers by the party's Central Office (also published in August 1980) reported growing disenchantment. And in October 1980 the Labour Party Conference voted overwhelmingly in support of withdrawal.

The essential fact is that whatever advantages the EEC may have for some of its members, the British economy can, on balance, only suffer from being in it. However, the EEC as a whole is undergoing a crisis. It was born in a period of world economic expansion with its core members like West Germany, France and Italy growing very fast. Its two main 'constructions' were the Common Agricultural Policy (CAP) and the Customs' Union, establishing by 1968 a common external tariff, reducing tariff barriers within the EEC. Since then the ending of the long boom, followed by economic crisis, has aggravated the differences in economic growth and the consequent and growing divergence in policies of EEC members. Britain joined the EEC on the eve of the world economic recession, not in very good condition, and when her *relative* performance over the previous two decades had been far from sparkling.

The dominant business and political circles in the UK were bankrupt of any other perspectives; they supported British entry and fought for it hoping that somehow they could 'use' it for their wider objectives. What arguments did they use to persuade the people and themselves that this was vital?

There were the *political* arguments. Britain was geographically close to Europe and had common political and military objectives with the EEC countries especially in a united front against the 'threat' from the Soviet Union. The future rested with powerful blocks and an enlarged EEC could begin to match the two superpowers (USA and USSR), taking into account also the growing strength of Japan and China. Moreover, since the EEC already existed and was coordinating policies, Britain's voice needed to be heard in its formulations.

Then there were the economic arguments. New markets for British agriculture would be opened up in Western Europe. The removal of tariffs between EEC countries meant that Britain would be part of a greatly enlarged market which would offer the possibilities of economies of scale, specialization and expansion. There would be costs, of course, but these would be more, far more, than offset by the dynamic advantages of membership.

In examining these arguments it is difficult to disentangle the attempt to deceive others from the self-deception of those who put them forward.

What has actually happened?

I am not proposing in this section to provide a history of events but rather to summarize some of the main effects of UK membership of the EEC. In the very broadest terms, membership of the EEC has *reinforced* the relative decline of UK industry.

First, the response of important groups of industrial and financial capital has been to invest far more heavily in the rest of the EEC where markets were expanding more rapidly. Their capital investment in the EEC grew faster than their exports to the EEC. In contrast, the exports of the other EEC countries to the UK grew faster than their investment in the UK. So the productive power, employment and exporting capacity of the UK has been weakened and that of other EEC countries strengthened.

Second, since Britain joined it has been estimated (*Cambridge Journal of Economics*, December 1979) that EEC manufacturers have succeeeded in increasing their penetration of the British market far more than British firms have managed to enter EEC markets. In 1978 the UK ran a deficit in *manufacturing* trade with the rest of the EEC of about

£2,000 million, most of it accounted for by trade with West Germany. Yet we depend on our manufacturing export surplus to finance our imports of foodstuffs and materials. In 1979 the overall deficit on all UK visible trade with the rest of the EEC rose to £2,750 million.

The rest of the EEC has become a more important trading partner for the UK, taking 42% of all UK exports and 45% of our imports. In sector after sector of manufacturing industry, British output is taking a beating from EEC imports. In some cases, as in chemicals, all the growth in the UK market is being taken by EEC imports.

Whereas it is very difficult to separate the specific impact of EEC membership from other factors, our third point is much clearer. Membership of the EEC and of CAP has obviously meant much higher food prices for British consumers. Higher prices have to be paid by food manufacturers and processors and, because we import much more of our food from non-EEC countries, the levies we put on these imports to bring them up to CAP prices is more of a burden to us than to other more self-sufficient EEC countries. And in so far as we import more of our food from the EEC we obviously pay the higher CAP prices.

This leads directly to our fourth point and the one which has been most in the news: the contribution the UK makes to the EEC budget. In 1980 Britain is estimated to be contributing £1,300 million to the Community budget. If we add to this the *excess* cost of food imports from the EEC (£300 million), the foreign exchange which the UK has to transfer to the EEC (after taking account of what we receive) was £1,600 million.*

Fifth, we have to recognize that the total outcome of our relations with the EEC in terms of transfers, trade deficits, and so forth, have repercussions on the growth and amount of Britain's national income. The effect is to slow down the overall growth of the economy and income, weaken our manufacturing base, reduce employment, and make the balance of payments more fragile. The *Cambridge Journal of Economics* estimated that in 1977/8 the total cost to real national income could have been as high as 15% amounting in 1977 prices to a loss of about £22 billion.

If we rested our argument only on these five counts, membership of the EEC has both aggravated already existing problems and created

---

* Britain's consumers in 1980 paid £2,250 million more for food because of the Common Market's high-price agricultural policy, according to a Ministry of Agriculture estimate (*Guardian*, 24/10/80).

additional ones (without taking any account of specific issues such as fishing policy).

Did the 'settlement' reached by Mrs Thatcher in spring 1980 change this picture? This is by no means clear cut. The settlement promised to transfer some of the budgetary burden to West Germany, *but*: it altered nothing on our first three counts and in these respects we may only expect the situation to worsen; and it did nothing to check the *growth* of the budgeting burden, so that in absolute terms Britain will find itself paying even more as the costs of CAP rise and the EEC runs out of money.

Moreover the EEC argues that the rebate to the UK must be for new projects of which it approves, i.e. it wishes to extend its control over areas of UK spending, and the 'agreement' was linked and remains linked with other issues such as raising food prices and future negotiations on energy policy (by which is meant availability of North Sea oil and its price to other EEC countries). None of these problems has been resolved.

If the British economy is to begin to climb out of its desperate state, it must rid itself of the handicaps imposed on it by EEC membership. But the EEC imposes still further limitations on any British government wishing to take an interventionist path.

The Treaty of Rome and the institutions of the EEC place many restrictions on government policy particularly on state aid to industry. The UK no longer has full control of commercial policy and this means that many major decisions about trade, in steel, shipbuilding and textiles, for instance, are in the hands of the EEC.

In turn this is part of a broader and more fundamental issue: the regulations passed by the Council of Ministers are applicable to the domestic law of the UK, and the European Court can decide on the effect of regulations on UK law, and of EEC treaties as they affect Britain. Parliament has been deprived of its sovereignty; a rising tide of EEC law is flowing through all areas of British life. Moreover, the Treaty of Rome is dedicated to the destruction of all obstacles to the free movement of capital and labour, to reducing state expenditure or support to industry, and to minimizing all barriers to free competition.

Nevertheless, could not the EEC be changed, transform itself? Is it necessary for Britain to leave the EEC if it wishes to follow the kind of alternative strategy we have outlined (or for that matter, a much more limited one)?

Should Britain leave the EEC?

Leaving the EEC is not a condition for beginning to change economic strategy and initiating policies of expansion. Many challenges have been made to the EEC and to the letter of the Treaty of Rome, especially by France and Italy, and accommodated to varying degrees. Large measures of protection by national governments are already practised and are being extended. In the current world situation national policies are bound to diverge or conflict, as the struggle over Britain's budgetary contribution and over the rising costs of CAP indicate. The negotiations for the entry of Spain, Greece and Portugal are already setting up new tensions because of the profound consequences for the EEC; strong reactions are evident in France and Italy.

Nevertheless, the full-scale application of our alternative strategy amounts to a rejection of the Treaty of Rome and the main assumptions behind the policies followed by the EEC Commission. The AES involves substantial extension of public ownership and public intervention, large-scale state-initiated and -supported investment programmes, strategic control of foreign trade, and the reinstatement of exchange controls. And all this not on a temporary basis but as part of a long-term strategy, assuming that it receives sufficient electoral support from the voters.

In addition, the reconstruction of the UK economy must mean getting rid of the direct and indirect costs of membership of the EEC which represent a large drain on our limited resources.

It seems unlikely that the EEC as presently constituted could accommodate this. It has an interest in British membership in the sense that Britain is a good market for its food surpluses and is a large contributor to the CAP. But these are amongst the very things which make the EEC unacceptable to the UK.

Could the EEC be reformed or are there important reasons for a left government, for instance, retaining membership? From some circles on the left the case for staying in is argued along the following lines.

The EEC, it is said, is a reality which is irreversible and corresponds to the forces for economic integration. Second, the scale of the problems facing Western Europe in such areas as control of the multinationals, high technology, energy and regional development, requires inter-governmental action which the EEC can facilitate. Third, national solutions for the working classes of individual countries are not possible; the EEC provides a framework for increasing solidarity and joint action between the socialist, communist, trade union and labour movements of the member countries.

It is very hard to see, at first sight, how these arguments stand up to the economic and political realities of the EEC. From the standpoint of the *people* of the UK and the need to throw off unnecessary burdens, Britain would need to be relieved of all financial responsibility for CAP, be able to follow an entirely different food importing and agricultural policy, be free to follow the main economic strategy of the AES, and assert the sovereignty of the House of Commons. Proposals to 'democratize' the EEC, including plans to strengthen the European Parliament, represent not so much extensions of democracy as the making more palatable of the removal of centres of decision-making further away from the people.

Intergovernmental cooperation does not depend on the existence of the EEC; other bodies exist and can be created for that purpose. Trade union and working-class cooperation has not been helped by the EEC; it is necessary independently of the EEC and needs to be worked for on a broader scale than that represented by nine or even twelve members of the EEC.

The specific needs of the UK, as compared with that of other EEC members, means that though the socialist and communist left in some EEC countries see the virtues of working within it, that is not the case in Britain.

What would we *lose* by leaving the EEC? Apart from the admittedly important point of no longer being involved in the decision-making bodies of the EEC, we should find the EEC external tariff applied to UK exports to EEC countries. That tariff, however, is 7% or less on manufactured goods and, in doing this, the EEC countries (*especially* West Germany) would have to consider what is to happen to their large exports to the UK. A bargain would probably be struck once the UK was able to use her bargaining power as a major market for manufactured goods and foodstuffs for EEC countries, and that – however modified – would still be true with an expanding British economy.

Britain would be free to consider a much wider perspective in trade with other countries, including the less-developed countries, as suggested in the previous chapter. Before entering the EEC the UK had an agricultural guaranteed price-support system with an annual price review which worked, and an extended network of commodity marketing boards (on the lines of the Milk Marketing Board) could be established.

Cooperation in the fields of aerospace with firms and governments in the EEC would still be possible; the giant multinationals often involved in such ventures are globally organized and take a world-view of their activities.

Joining the EEC in the first place was an act of political bankruptcy in which the full-scale consequences were miscalculated and have proved costly. Leaving it would be a positive advantage.

8 A New Social Strategy

I WHAT DO WE WANT?

The Tory Government has set its sights on dismantling the 'welfare state' as it was constructed after 1945. It is doing this not because it cannot afford it, though that is what it says, but because it is *hostile* to it in principle. The severity of its attack is beginning to be understood; as in other fields, resistance will grow, but it often takes the form of demanding a return to the position before May 1979. I shall argue that this is a mistake: we cannot go back and we should not try to. But I want first not just to list what the Tories are doing and proposing to do, but explain why they have been able to do it.

The Government from the beginning has set itself the aim of cutting public spending in *real* terms and as a proportion of GDP. The attack is heaviest over aid to industry, lending to nationalized industries, and expenditure on housing, roads, transport, and education, whereas big increases are to be made in defence and law and order. The Tory Government has used a policy of severe cash limits to try to impose its plans. Moreover, a mass of major legislation has now been passed or is on its way which directly affects the social and welfare services. This includes: ending the linking of retirement pensions to the earnings of people at work; reducing the real value of benefits for sickness, maternity, invalidity and unemployment; reducing, and then abolishing, the earnings-related supplement; reducing unemployment benefit still further for those drawing occupational pensions; refusing to maintain the value of child benefit, and of children's increases in National Insurance benefits; and vindictively penalizing strikers' families.

This is of course far from a complete catalogue; no area of welfare, planning or local government is untouched by a reactionary tidal wave intended not to take Britain back to some Victorian era but to carry it forward to some *new* place. The Social Services correspondent of *The Times* (21/5/1980) wrote that 'the aim of providing freedom from want through a national insurance system is about to receive its most serious blow since the founding of the modern welfare state'.

But what is the intention of Thatcherism? It is sometimes presented as the withdrawal of the state from spheres it should not meddle with – a weakening, as it may seem, of the role of the state. It would be more accurate to describe it as the vigorous and systematic use of the power of the state to set severe limits on the public provision of social and welfare services, and to oblige people to deal with services and welfare as individuals and family units which are to be *private* not social or public concerns. Success or failure, poverty or wealth, employment or unemployment, are to be seen as the outcome of what individuals do or fail to do. Therefore the distribution of wealth, the scale of inequality, the existence of large numbers of poor people and of millions of unemployed are to be seen not as political and social questions but personal and private. And those instruments of the state (such as the forces of law and order) which are necessary to enforce such a code and ensure that the consequences do not erupt into the public domain are to be strengthened in resources and status.

That part of the Tory argument which argues that the cuts are needed to bring down the PSBR as a necessary condition of bringing down inflation, has been dealt with in Chapters 3 and 4. In the following few paragraphs, I want only to relate the actual measures of the Government to some of its arguments and objectives.

First, the forcing of people to accept lower wages than they believe are 'fair'. Employers complain that workers can get more from unemployment pay and social security than the wages they are offering. Workers, it is said, are in danger of pricing themselves out of work. The reduction in *real* value of benefits (the first attempt in fifty years) is but one of the measures.

Second, in the name of increasing the individual's freedom to choose whether to spend money, a powerful squeeze is being imposed on the National Health Service. Clinical and some other services are to be contracted out to the private sector, hospital closures enforced, and the climate created for the growth of private medicine. Nearly 3 million people are now covered by private medical insurance and that includes many groups of manual workers in schemes such as those negotiated by the Electricians' Union. The *Lancet*, Britain's main medical journal, attacked the government's proposals as 'irrelevant, ignorant, suspect and wanton' (*Guardian*, 23/8/1980).

Third, in education, the abandonment of comprehensive education as an aim is symbolized by the 'Assisted Places Scheme', giving the independent schools £70 million of public money to educate a selected group of students from the state sector, and encouraging the extension of private education.

Fourth, in the name of encouraging enterprise, tax changes have given gains of £1·5 billion to the top 7% of taxpayers.

And fifth, as we have already noted, a considerable redirection of resources is to go to military spending and on 'law and order'.

These are only illustrations of the scale of the attack which, in addition, took place at a time when the Government seriously underestimated the rise in unemployment and the additional costs that would impose on government spending. It certainly did not reckon on the additional costs in ill health (mental and physical), vandalism, and crime, which that unemployment would give rise to over the coming years. Moreover, the number of elderly people in the population will increase by $3\frac{1}{2}$% between 1979 and 1983, representing a big additional demand for resources.

As in other matters, the prospects are grim; but how did this come about? Were the roots of the present problem in the very way in which the welfare state was constructed and constrained, *not just financially but also in conception?*

The welfare state, as we have known it, is mainly the product of the social reform and anti-fascist movement that acquired tremendous force during the Second World War and which obliged the Tory Party to adapt itself to it. A consensus was established between the leaders of the Labour, Tory and Liberal parties for full employment as an objective of government policy and the construction of a wide-ranging system of welfare and social security. This was easier to pursue then because the British economy grew faster than it had done previously and took part in a prolonged period of world capitalist expansion.

This consensus, however, was for a welfare system that would, as far as possible, not threaten capitalist relationships. The basic principle of the famous Beveridge Plan – security of want without a means test – was *not* fully carried out (as Ruth Lister of Child Poverty Action Group rightly pointed out, quoting Beveridge's own point that 'a permanent scale of [insurance] benefit below subsistence, assuming supplementation on a means test as a normal feature, cannot be defended') (quoted in Blake and Ormerod, 1980, pp. 201–2).

The pervasive and dominant role of class in undermining the advance of the social services can be illustrated from a working party report set up by the Department of Health and Social Security (DHSS) in 1977 and published in August 1980. Comparing unskilled workers and their families with those of professional workers, the report found that unskilled workers die younger, suffer more from bronchitis, TB and lung cancer, and keep fewer of their own teeth. Twice as many of the wives in that category died in childbirth and four times as many of their children in infancy. Many of these differences extend to wider categories of manual workers than the unskilled and their families. *If the mortality rate of the professional class had applied to the unskilled and semi-skilled in 1970–2, 74,000 lives of people under 75 would not have been lost, including nearly 10,000 children and 32,000 men* [sic] *of working age.*

It goes almost without saying that the Tory Government rejected the proposals of the DHSS working party on the grounds of cost. Although, after more than twenty-five years of welfare expansion and reform, this is a particularly poignant illustration, other studies in the education system and on the extent of poverty bring out the existence of further great and persistent inequalities and deprivation. Estimates made in 1977 suggested that six million people were in poverty.

The weakening position of the British capitalist economy as described in Chapter 2 gave rise to increasing pressure to modify the scale of the welfare and social security system; from the mid-seventies especially, government policies made it more and more difficult to meet existing standards quite apart from the growing needs and expectations of people.

In addition, the whole structure of the social services (e.g. of the education and health services) was innately bureaucratic. Within schools, head-teachers enjoyed extraordinary powers; within the health services, the medical profession dominated practice and approach; throughout, the consumers of these services were in the role of clients, and the majority of those working in the services were excluded from any serious part in policy and decision making.

Any debate on education and welfare provision, where it took place, was preoccupied mainly with resources, and not with the services' content or organization, or with the need to consult and involve the workers or the public who used them in their running. *How much* education not *what kind of* education; *how much* money for the health service not *what kind of* service. In the social security system where the disadvantaged and the deprived were especially involved, the situation was even more dismal and, overall, the power of the welfare apparatus to challenge the values of the system was blunted.

In practice, as distinct from the passing of resolutions, the trade unions and the labour movement have been slow to recognize the threat they faced from the attacks on the public sector. The *social wage* (i.e. services received by way of central and local government) has often been taken too much for granted and given too little weight in the campaigning of the movement. There was insufficient recognition that discontent was growing amongst large bodies of people, largely unorganized in unions, and with the way the social welfare services were structured and operated. Amongst wage earners there was a feeling that the rising burden of taxation imposed on them by the government through inflation was not improving their real take-home pay, or being compensated for by the services they used.

This was the situation, as stated in Chapter 3, which Thatcherism was able to exploit. A campaign based on returning to some *status quo* would therefore be a serious error.

Britain needs a new social strategy. What should be its character? Nothing is easier in this field than rhetoric and promises. Massive resources are needed but in addition hardly less massive changes in public opinion and political will. These paragraphs are concerned with *direction* but the reader will see that some of the proposals are indeed immediate campaigning issues. Two concepts could sum up the direction: *equal access* and *democratization*.

The important point about democratization is not a *formal* democratic structure but the active and continuous involvement of people in the way the services work and their content. For instance, in education (leaving aside further and higher education), the campaign to fight the Tory cuts should create a movement – i.e. committees, organizations and alliances – which begin to intervene in local government policy on education, making the local education authorities both more representative and responsive. Within the schools the dominance of the head should be removed by the formation of school councils representing teachers, students, parents and ancillary workers (whoever has experienced a real partnership in operation between the 'dinner ladies', caretaker, teachers and school secretaries – as happens in some schools – has had a foretaste of what even this limited cooperation can achieve). Furthermore, all these forces combined need to be involved in a public discussion on the content of education, curricula and systems of examination. If schools are to help prepare their students to confront the rapidly changing world they live in and help to change it, to overcome racialist and sexist ideas, then not only new resources but new ideas are crucial.

In the health service the immediate campaigning proposals are obvious enough, including the opposition to private insurance schemes.

Out of these campaigns to frustrate the Tory attack must also develop a broad movement which pursues the need for a democratic structure around reconstructed health authorities and within the institutions (hospitals, etc.). The aim should be a service directed at prevention and positive improvement of the health of the people. The patient–doctor relationship has been especially damaging to women (as the feminist movement has continually argued), in the way women are 'handled' in hospitals and clinics.

In every sphere labour movement and community organizations, together with those professionally involved, must find ways of cooperating in both formulating policies and carrying them through.

These remarks obviously relate to the principle of equal access; the practical meaning is to remove the discrimination on grounds of class, sex, age and race which now pervades the system. Even within our economy as it stands, but still more in an expanding one, there are strong reasons why not just the absolute amount of resources but an increasing *share* should go to meet the needs of the people in a collective way through welfare services, health, education, leisure, cultural and sports facilities. The same argument applies to housing and transport. Such social provision will enrich society as a whole, open up and provide opportunities for the greatest number, and redistribute resources so that the less advantaged can gain. It will also facilitate the provision – where necessary – of positive discrimination for ethnic minorities and any groups so disadvantaged and discriminated against that only positive action to bring them forward can redress their situation.

There are thus good reasons for not using the term 'social wage'. The phrase has a useful meaning but it is too limited. We need a wider view which takes account of the millions who are not wage workers and are not involved with wage negotiations.

Though this is not the place for detailed programmes, an exception needs to be made for two sets of proposals – those which affect the poor and the low paid and those concerning women's rights. In the case of the former, demands include – first – a national minimum wage of, say, two thirds of average earnings; second, adequate non-means-tested benefits to those unable to work; third, an increase in the *real* value of child benefits.

In the case of women's rights the proposals endorsed at the 1980 Labour Party Conference provide a good summary: an end to the separation of women into low-paid job categories; an end to tax and social security discriminations; the provision of nursery or workplace crèche facilities for every child, including those whose mothers work unsocial hours; two months' fully paid maternity-leave before, and seven months' after, the birth of a child; equal access to all academic and practical subjects at school; increased facilities for birth-control; a ban on all forced sterilization; private abortion clinics to be incorporated into the NHS; abortions free of charge; abortion day-care facilities; and free counselling on contraception, pregnancy-testing, abortion, sterilization and fertility.

In a new social strategy, the combined forces of the labour movement, community bodies, women's organizations, ethnic minorities and others must formulate a programme which will change the position of women in society, overcome the discrimination experienced by ethnic minorities, and create an entirely different environment for the 16–19 age group than the one they now face. The movement to throw back the Tory onslaught cannot therefore, and should not, be separated from the struggle to change the direction and character of the 'welfare state'.

It is impossible to separate proposals for a new welfare strategy from the way it is financed. In any case, a key part of such a social strategy is its attack on the severe inequalities that come from the concentration of capital in a few hands. These are the topics that concern Section II.

II   CAN WE AFFORD IT?

The Tory Government has seized hold of a whole battery of notions to justify its attack on the welfare system and its attempts to both cut and redirect government spending. One of its most popular arguments has been that the high level of government spending in the past has 'crowded out' the private firms, soaking up labour and funds and, as a result, increased the burden of taxation on firms and individuals. A second argument is that the 'excessive' burden of taxation discourages people from working hard and showing enterprise.

If comparisons with other countries are relevant, there is no case to answer. On the first 'charge', Britain's public spending as a proportion of GDP was almost *exactly average* for the twelve major countries of the OECD in both the mid-fifties and the mid-seventies. As for the excessive growth of public spending, Britain stood in a group of seven countries whose spending increased by a third between those dates. Seven other countries had increased their public spending at a higher rate, and only three other countries had lower rates of growth in their public spending.

Moreover, most of the countries had grown faster than the UK, so even if it were true that public spending uses up resources which could allow the private sector to expand, there is no support for the argument that cuts in public spending will stimulate investment to fill the gap. In 1974/5 the public sector borrowing requirement was at a peak of 9·1% of GDP. In 1979/80 it was down to 5·1%. Investment and output have hardly prospered; in fact, the public spending cuts have damaged investment by cutting the level of demand.

The charge of excessive taxation is also misplaced. In the case of direct taxes (personal income tax plus employees' social security contributions), Britain is again virtually on the average for the same twelve countries. There is no independent evidence that the difference in taxation between Britain and other countries have affected incentives.

There is a third, rather more 'vicious', argument which is that unemployment has risen mainly because of higher unemployment benefits and social security. All our unemployed, it seems, are volunteers for the idle life. Here again, there is no serious case to answer. If some economists (not to mention Tory politicians) cannot see with their own eyes that a continuing crisis combined with policies of rationalization has reduced the numbers of those employed whilst at the same time the labour force is increasing, then economics has indeed become a 'dismal science'.

The Tory campaign against public spending has fostered an atmosphere of guilt by daily hammering home the proposition in the mass media that the country is like a 'housewife' who spends more than her income. This argument is dealt with in Chapter 4. But if public spending is not an ogre, it cannot simply be expanded at will. There are limits to the amount a government can take back in taxation and on the amounts it can borrow. In that sense, the demand that those who advance major proposals for public spending should say how they are to be financed is justified. My answer will nevertheless be in general terms because I have not attempted to put forward a specific set of propositions which are to be implemented within, say, a four-year period. At the end of the book, the reader will find some estimates in the Appendix and also references to books and pamphlets where further estimates have been made. My concern here is to indicate in broad terms where the resources for such a programme could be found.

In any given period of time a government spending-programme must have its priorities; the resources that might be available will depend on whether the government starts from a position of unemployed people and machines or a condition of full employment and capacity working. First, resources will come from the growth of the economy and the rising number of employed and the smaller number of unemployed. This means higher levels of personal income and profits, and therefore buoyant tax revenues from firms and individuals; and lower expenditures by government on unemployment pay, social security and the other costs to government of economic crisis.

Second, economic growth would increase the rate at which productivity improves. This would be very fast when the economy is recovering from a crisis; but it would be the *main* source of growth once an economy was fully employed.

Third, certain types of government spending such as military expenditure can be cut. Defence spending has been increasing as a percentage of GDP and is certainly out of line with, for instance, EEC countries and Japan. Even on pessimistic estimates, savings of not less than £500 million a year over five years would be available but they could be far greater. (The lunatic scheme for a future £5,000 million programme on Trident missiles would be abandoned.)

Fourth, the UK is lucky to have the revenues from North Sea oil. By raising North Sea oil prices in line with OPEC, the Government is in practice imposing a massive indirect tax on all consumers of oil (direct and indirect). Combined tax revenues from North Sea oil and gas could reach £30 billion by 1985.

The Government could of course reduce this indirect tax, but these very large revenues could be used for the industrial regeneration of Britain and not for a pre-election tax-cutting spree by the Tory Government as it approaches election year in 1984. That revenue could be still further increased by extending public ownership, in which case less profit from North Sea oil would go overseas. Looked at more widely, the way the spending programmes of central and local government are financed is inseparable from the degree of democratic control and changes in the distribution of wealth. Some *redistribution* between classes and groups and also between spending programmes will also have a part to play.

Reforming the tax system

There is some agreement amongst social reformers that the poor should be exempted from tax and that those who have higher incomes should pay proportionately more. The UK tax system, even before the 1979

Budget, was at best only slightly 'progressive', if at all, in that sense. This is because of two special factors. One was inflation which brought millions into the tax net and increased the proportion of taxable incomes (i.e. the Government was able to increase taxes without legislation!); the other is the system of allowances which benefited the better-off as against the poorest (e.g. relief on mortgage interest payments and life assurance premiums). The redistribution, in so far as it happened at all, is more a redistribution within classes rather than from the rich to the poor; the benefits from the services provided by government go more to the better-off than the poorer groups in society.

A further result of inflation was to increase the share of direct as against indirect taxes in government revenue. The Tory Government certainly tackled this with a vengeance when it increased VAT, increased charges from the nationalized industries, and gave substantial tax benefits to the richest 7% of the taxpayers. The regressive element in the tax system was therefore increased.

What kind of tax policy would the AES require? First, with regard to direct and indirect taxation. The approach would involve: excluding the poor from the tax system; introducing reduced bands of rising tax rates for those who are above the exemption limit; ending personal allowance in their present form (i.e. reviewing present allowances on mortgage and life assurance payments – they could apply only up to a certain standard figure).

There is a case for abolishing the national insurance contribution which is a highly regressive tax hitting the poor hardest. But this would be a radical reform with major consequences. Perhaps national insurance contributions could be merged with income tax and put on a progressive basis or, as the TUC suggests, they could be made tax deductible.

Pending an alternative to VAT, zero or low VAT ratings should be extended on some essential goods; the rate on luxuries could be increased; a basic cheap fuel allowance could be introduced with rising charges for extra consumption.

Far harder to deal with is the present enormous dependence on income from duties on petrol, tobacco and alcohol, which in 1976/7 raised more money than VAT! Short of some revolution in the entire tax structure, this is not something that can be swiftly changed; it depends heavily on public attitudes and understanding of the problems created by pollution, smoking and over-drinking.

When it comes to corporate taxation, in 1977 Britain was about average in the proportion of total taxes that come from companies in major capitalist countries. But as a proportion of GDP it was amongst the *lowest*. As a result of government reliefs, many large companies pay little or no 'mainstream' tax (i.e. on their operational income). And much of the taxation that does take place is normally passed on to the consumer in higher prices. In addition there is widespread avoidance and evasion.

Corporate tax does not represent the saviour for public spending, but in an expanding economy with rising output and increased profit levels companies must be expected to make a substantial tax contribution. Reforms that could be considered include: progressive tax rates for larger companies; stringent treatment of costs, expenses and fringe benefits. Planning agreements with the largest companies would deal with transfer pricing and the use of tax havens to avoid taxes; and investment grants could be given for specific schemes to discourage unnecessary or wasteful investment (not all investment is good investment!).

The second main issue in tax reform is one of the most central problems for strengthening democracy: the financing of local authorities. These at the moment account for more than 11% of GDP, 40% of public spending on goods and services, raise 9% of government revenue in the form of rates, and employ 12% of the country's labour force. Increasingly, governments have sought to limit the autonomy of local authorities; their dependence on central government financing has grown. Apart from income from fees and charges which account for 20% of local government spending, 40% comes from rates and 60% from central government grants. The new Local Government Bill proposes not only to control local government borrowing, but the amount local authorities can spend. Through the introduction of a new block grant to replace the help previously given to poor local authorities or those in special circumstances, the government intends to acquire power to penalize local authorities which overspend according to some standard figure.

If local authorities are not just to be agents of central government, they need a far more independent source of income. The rating system, however, is itself a very regressive tax and full of anomalies. The major alternatives are a sales tax as a local indirect tax on expenditure, or a local income tax on personal income. Because a sales tax is difficult to operate, involving additional costly administration, a local incomes tax (based on progressive principles) offers the best approach. Local authorities could set their own tax rate, but the overall burden of taxation need not increase because central government could reduce its own tax-take to compensate. Unless a reform of this kind is introduced, the cost of services must increasingly fall on central government and local authorities will lose any vestige of local democracy.

We come in the third place to one of the objectives of the AES: the reduction in the unequal distribution of wealth. Large concentrations of personal wealth represent sources of power; and there is an offence to human dignity in the coexistence of immense affluence alongside degrading poverty. The position we now have is that the top 20% of the population owns 80% of Britain's wealth – nearly as much as fifty years ago. Furthermore, *the bulk of the wealth of the very richest comes from inheritance.*

There is a case therefore for a wealth tax. Many other capitalist economies have such a tax in one form or another. The objective should be to reduce the largest wealth holdings and thereby contribute to greater equality. This means adding income tax and the tax on wealth so that the combined payments can come close to or even exceed 100% of the disposable income derived from the wealth (it should be, that is, an *additive* tax). It must strike particularly at large-scale inherited wealth and treat capital gains as income.

Such are some of the elements of a radical tax and fiscal policy which is a necessary part of the overall social strategy dealt with in this chapter. Such a new social strategy does not amount to the elimination of the rich or of capitalists as a class. However, in the conditions of Britain it represents, if pursued, a shift in political, social and economic relationships. And for this to happen changes in attitude must take place not only amongst those directly involved in the institutions, but primarily amongst millions of people.

9 How Do We Get There?

Introduction

The Alternative Economic Strategy is and must be a programme of radical reform. It does not and should not require those who support it to be committed to a socialist reconstruction of Britain. If we are not clear on this we shall abandon one of its main sources of strength, namely that it is a 'common programme' being constructed by many different groups and interests.

But is there a connection between the struggle for the radical policies of the AES and the struggle for socialism in Britain? It should be obvious that the proposals put forward in this book cannot be inserted into the old system like a new fuse in an old fuse-box. Any attempt to carry them through must alter the way the system works and open it up to even more fundamental changes. The reason socialists and communists have played such an active (though in no sense exclusive) part in putting the AES together is because they recognize the pressures in the system which produce the crisis, and the *direction* in which change must be made. Certainly, they see the AES as part of a strategy for such change.

In the campaign to win support for the AES there should be a developing and lively discussion between socialists and non-socialists in which the nature of capitalism and the necessity for a new kind of social system based on production for need, co-operation and democratic involvement, is argued out. That argument will be most fruitful if it is carried on in conditions where millions of people are involved in struggle for the common programme and its individual demands.

However, amongst those who describe themselves as socialists or social democrats, there are two groupings who oppose the AES for very different reasons. On the one hand there is the right wing within the labour and trade union movement, currently represented by Denis Healey, David Owen, and William Rodgers within the Parliamentary Labour Party (PLP), and Frank Chapple and Sydney Weighell within the trade unions, all of whom wish to continue the tradition of Wilson and Callaghan. This group considers the AES to be a revolutionary programme with which it profoundly disagrees. On the other are leftist groups such as *Militant* (operating within the Labour Party) and the

Socialist Workers' Party, who believe the AES is a reformist programme which should be rejected by the labour movement. Each of these needs to be dealt with before we move on to a discussion of the 'mainstream' left represented by those around Tony Benn, *Tribune*, the Communist Party, and trade union leaders like Bernard Dix, Clive Jenkins, Bob Wright, Alan Fisher and Arthur Scargill who regard themselves as committed socialists and see the AES not only as a vital alternative to Toryism but as integral to the struggle for socialism.

A reply to the right wing in the labour movement

The right wing can be dealt with briefly because in Chapter 3 the practice and policies of the 1974–9 Labour Government were critically reviewed. The positions of Callaghan and Healey have not changed since 1979; they have not repudiated or criticized their own policies when in government. Of course, in opposition and in the light of the Tory onslaught, they are obliged to adopt an anti-Tory posture, attacking Thatcherism for being too radical, proposing a relaxation of monetary constraints, arguing for a rise in the Public Sector Borrowing Requirement during the recession, proposing the use of North Sea oil revenues to cut VAT, calling for a reduction in interest rates, and acknowledging that selective and temporary import controls may be necessary. The right wingers can hardly propose to lead the Labour Party into an election against Thatcherism with a Thatcherist manifesto, so they will go along with suitably qualified phrases about economic expansion, reducing unemployment, introducing industrial democracy and also pledging to repeal the Employment Act.

It is hard to see how this constitutes an economic strategy different to that pursued during the last Labour Government. If this book is right in arguing that British capitalism has entered deeper and more turbulent waters, then simply modifying the worst extremes of Thatcherism will not take us far. Perhaps they gamble on an upturn of the economic cycle and the availability of oil revenues to give them some tactical space, but on a longer view they would be obliged to move radically to the right or to the left.

Their opposition to the AES is not a matter of technical economic analysis but arises from a particular view of society and of socialism.

Their concept of socialism is bounded by the idea of 'equality' which they see as arising mainly from tax and welfare policies (as in education), but not from ending the dominance of capital. As the difficulties of British capitalism increased, they abandoned even the pursuit of equality. They have certainly moved a long way from the 'naïve' position that state intervention equals socialism, but their solution is a 'mixed economy' with such greatly reduced emphasis on public ownership and intervention that the concerns of big business inevitably predominate.

They hold a formalist approach to democracy based on the principle: 'elect us to get on with the job' or, in the more pungent words of Jim Callaghan in 1977, 'back us or sack us'. Their opposition to democratic reform within the Labour Party is consistent with this. What unnerves them is a popular grass-roots' movement and participation. They therefore tend to exaggerate (as do many others not on the right) the role of Parliament, even though it is becoming clearer to many that power has been greatly concentrated in the Cabinet, and often in small caucuses, reinforced by a powerful system of patronage controlled by the Prime Minister; and that the top personnel of the civil service, judiciary, armed forces and police are deeply attached to the establishment.*

It is not hard to see that the approach of the right wingers led them to the very thing they say they are critical of: a bureaucratic, non-democratic public sector. The disillusion this has produced, and which was useful to Thatcherism, is now brought forward by them as a justification for avoiding any radical changes. The right is *not* searching for more popular and democratic ways of transforming our society.

It argues that in any case the AES does not command popular support (an issue discussed later in the chapter). This is in order to back up the familiar argument that the Labour Party can win elections only by occupying the 'middle ground' and winning support from the 'floating voter'. But what decides where the 'middle ground' is? A political party without a sense of direction can hardly inspire wide support; one has only to compare the defensive way in which the right wing led Labour into the 1979 election with the intense ideological campaign conducted by the Tory party. The policy must obviously spring from the concerns of the people, but the extent to which the Labour Party, the trade unions

---

* The number of senior civil servants who on retirement have joined the boards of big companies, often in areas they were involved with when in government service, has become a matter of public concern. Examples include: Admiral Sir Edward Ashmore, Chief of Defence Staff, moving to Racal Electronics; Sir Leslie Murphy, Assistant Secretary, Ministry of Fuel and Power, moving to Mobil; Stanley Wright, Under-Secretary at the Treasury, moving to Lazards (merchant bankers who are part of the Cowdray group).

and all other sections of the movement campaign for it, winning support and constructing alliances, will *shift* the ground on which political battles are fought. It can limit the territory available to the Liberal and Nationalist Parties, as well as to the Tories.

The right wing is in difficulties partly because Thatcherism has dealt a severe blow to the consensus in which it shared; and now the radicalism of the Tories has reinforced changes already taking place amongst activists within the labour movement. The 1980 Labour Party Conference indicated a new balance of power which represents a serious threat to the right wing. For decades its dominance was not seriously challenged. It was buttressed by the 'insulation' of the PLP from the party conference, by the election of the leader by the PLP, and by the concentration of effective policy-making in the hands of the parliamentary leadership and not in the party conference or in the party's National Executive Committee (NEC). The Constituency Labour Parties (CLPs) have been primarily concerned with elections, barely involved their membership, and were largely 'non-political' in their everyday activity. In addition, the CLPs have often been separated from any industrial connections on the one hand and from Labour groups in local authorities on the other.

This has amounted to a powerful system of control. However, the anxieties of the right have, with good reason, grown in recent years, especially because of changes in mood which arose from Labour's defeats in 1970 and 1979. Under the impact of the 1970 defeat and a wave of industrial struggles, the left was able to win the 1973 Labour Party Conference for a radical programme which embodied much of what is now discussed as the AES. The 1974–9 Labour Government in essence repudiated that programme, but the radical positions, confirmed also in the 1976 party conference, provided a running critique of the government and a basis for challenging right-wing policies. In addition, the traditional dominance of the right in the major trade unions has become insecure. Moreover at the 1980 Labour Party Conference a major challenge was made to the power of the PLP, seeking to change the way the party leader is elected, and attempting to assert the policy-making supremacy of the party conference and NEC.

A struggle to democratize the Labour Party is thus under way. A new situation is coming into being, though right-wing Labour ideas together with those of Thatcherism still dominate popular thinking and constitute the main problem for the left in influencing millions of people. However, within the left itself there is also a leftist tendency which considers it a major task to discredit the AES. Because of the confusion this can cause, a reply is necessary.

A reply to the leftists

So far from being a revolutionary programme (as the right wing believe), the leftists regard the AES as reformist and collaborationist. They see its aim as the regeneration of capitalism, making it work more efficiently. In addition, it is said to be chauvinist and nationalist, regarding the British crisis as unique instead of as part of a world capitalist crisis to which there cannot be a British solution. The AES, the leftists claim, proposes to tear Britain out of the world economy, or alternatively to make British capitalism more competitive as well as more protectionist. And they argue that this nationalist view diverts from the need for international mobilization since the only real answer is *world* socialism.

The leftists go on to argue that in any case the AES cannot work because it will be unacceptable to the capitalists (a criticism also made by the right), and because the measures proposed are insufficient to do what it promises; attempts to implement it would produce severe inflation, a profit squeeze, would provoke sabotage from capital nationally and internationally, and set the stage for a Chile-type solution. The Labour Party, argue the same people, can only betray the working class since it is a capitalist party, trapped by parliamentarism and reformism. As for the trade unions, they are run by bureaucrats.

Given the sharpness of their attack, what do the leftists offer instead? They argue that only those proposals may be advanced which threaten the system and demonstrate to the masses, if fought for, that socialism is the only answer. In leftist literature there is a weird mixture of 'immediate demands' such as the 35-hour week, and for 'opening the books', cutting military expenditure, and placing a limit on interest rates – which are hardly revolutionary – and demands for nationalizing the two hundred largest monopolies, and the whole financial system, and for the immediate adoption of a system of socialist planning – proposals which obviously require a socialist revolution.

In their criticisms the leftists exploit the fact that the AES is a 'common programme', involving many different theoretical and political positions – some, for instance, much closer to Keynesianism, others committedly Marxist. It is worth indicating three specific ways in which their approach differs from the strategic vision behind this book. The first difference is over the nature of revolutionary change in 'ad-

vanced' capitalist society. The leftists are still stuck with the model of
the revolutionary uprising of the Russian October Revolution of 1917.
A revolutionary situation comes about because of mounting class
struggle leading, for instance, to a general strike which will create a
chaotic situation in which the capitalist class cannot rule. In the course
of this struggle, new bodies are built up which are centres of workers'
power (giving rise to a situation of 'dual power'). If a revolutionary
party is present and sufficiently strong it can lead the workers to seize
state power, upon which these 'new bodies' (workers' councils or
soviets) become the foundation of the new socialist state.

There are many difficulties with this view. It tends to envisage
modern capitalist societies as cauldrons of discontent only contained by
a conspiracy between right-wing social democrats and big business: the
content of the cauldron boils over and, with the revolutionary party at
its head, blows off the lid. But this is not what such societies are like.
They are in fact extremely complex systems, bound by a network of institutions and relationships. They do not stand still but have undergone
a process of adaptation, arising — among other things — from the
struggle by the labour and democratic movements for the needs of the
people. They are class societies but they are stratified in many different
ways depending on their histories. Their political and social structures
show great variety and different degrees of adaptability (compare, for
instance, Japan and Sweden). The organizations of the working class in
these countries vary enormously in the extent to which they are united,
have political or religious affiliations, are closely linked with other
sections of the people, and so on. *People do not exist as 'workers-in-
factories' who only require to be told the truth about their exploitation
to recognize their 'real interests'.*

If this is so, revolution must be thought of much more as a prolonged
process. It will have its critical moments, but it can only be carried
through as a result of determined struggles on every single front to win
positions of advantage which in turn become the base for new advances.

The fantasies of most leftist groups are compounded by their idea
that even breaking through in one country would be insufficient to start
building socialism: that can only happen, they believe, if the
revolutionary uprising extends to other countries so that it becomes
successful on an international level. The chance of such virtually
simultaneous successful revolutions happening in all or most major
capitalist societies is so far-fetched as to postpone hope of radical
change in any one country to eternity. Radical change in one country

will influence the international climate in which other countries operate, but the *focus* of democratic struggle within each country is bound to be its own nation-state.

A second difficulty of the leftist view has to do with the nature of the 'state'. The leftists see the state as an entirely capitalist instrument which must be 'smashed', including the system of parliamentary and local government and all other apparatuses, including presumably those of education and welfare, and certainly the armed forces, police and judiciary as they now exist.

How is all this 'smashing' to take place in, for instance, British, West German or American societies? Sometimes there are suggestions that mass struggle will create conditions of 'chaos' in which presumably the armed forces and the police will be unable to function. There may even be notions of building up counter-military forces, though these are not normally expressed. The simple identification of the entire state apparatus with big business is false. As a result of prolonged struggles by the labour and democratic movement as well as arising from the needs of capitalists to cope with their own problems, the state has become a vast network involved in every aspect of people's lives; a 'place' where the democratic struggle is and needs to be conducted in addition to all other forms of struggle.

A special target for leftist criticism is reserved for those who believe that existing representative institutions, such as parliament, are important and can be transformed and used for democratic advance. Against this, the leftists counterpose 'mass democracy' and 'joint shop stewards committees' which will be the embryonic organs of workers' power, flowering into soviets or workers' councils, replacing parliament and local authorities. I too believe that to think that radical changes which threaten the domination of big business can simply be legislated by the House of Commons is illusory. An electoral victory is crucial, but, unless large numbers of people in their organizations campaign and actively support such changes with all their strength, a parliamentary approach would be revealed as hollow. A representative institution like the House of Commons partly reflects the balance of forces that has been established in a society. However, *it is itself a factor in that balance because of the role millions of people are prepared to allow it.*

Our present system of representative institutions is inadequate because much of the decision making and negotiations between centres of power necessarily takes place outside parliament. But the idea of factory-based workers' councils as the ideal form of organization is an

extremly narrowing and sectarian vision which is bound to be deeply
resented by the millions who do not work in such enterprises.

Leftists draw a sharp distinction between 'reformist' and
'revolutionary' demands, and between 'reforms' and 'revolution'. In the
prolonged and daily battle that goes on in enterprises and localities to
retain and increase some degree of democratic control, the improvements or reforms which are won are wherever possible in-
coporated into agreements, regulations, legislation (where desirable).
As this happens, it is true that the danger always exists that the struggle
itself will ebb and the gains then be whittled away. But what dis-
tinguishes the reformist from the revolutionary is that, for the latter, the ·
gains are seen as points from which to advance towards a fundamental
change in the class and property relationships in society. The role which
any given demand will play depends on the circumstances: 'bread and
peace' may be revolutionary in one set of conditions and lead to reforms
(only modifying the social structure) in another.

The failure to see revolutionary change as a process and not a single
decisive event leads the leftists to undervalue the importance of alliances
and to fail to recognize the stages in such a process.

Could a left-wing Labour government survive?

Let us suppose a Labour government has been elected on a programme
which contains substantial elements of the AES and feels committed to
carrying this programme through. It is possible that such a government
will emerge only after the British people have gone through the
experience of another centre-right Labour, if not another Tory
government. Much will depend on what is learned from these
experiences, and the degree to which a conscious desire for radical
change has been created and new points of advantage for further
change established. An electoral victory for the left cannot come from a
demoralized and defeated labour movement.

Popular support for a government committed to the AES will be the
more solid and durable the more the campaign for such a strategy has
changed the way in which people think and act – the more it has
captured their imagination as a different view of how they should live.
The future of such a strategy depends, in other words, on the creation of
a radical democratic outlook. This is vital if we consider some of the
problems such a government could face.

The most obvious ones arise from the hostility of big business and
reactionary forces both at home and internationally (discussed below).

But there is another less widely-discussed danger. This is that such a government would also arouse enormous expectations which cannot all be fulfilled and certainly not all be met with speed. A programme which involves massive new investment, renewal and expansion of social services, and an attack on poverty and inequality, cannot meet all the needs of the people for a substantial and all round rapid rise in real personal incomes. If high expectations combine with difficulties that might come from hostility and sabotage, as well as with other temporary setbacks, there could be a loss of popular support which would be systematically exploited by opponents of social change. So unless millions of people have a sober and realistic view about the short-term possibilities, and approve the main direction of change, support and the alliances which buttress it, will be divided.

One point should be made particularly clear. If the attempt to carry through such a programme loses popular support, such a government should be prepared to 'go to the country' and submit itself to the electoral verdict. To press ahead with a programme of radical change with insufficient popular support and inadequate alliances is a recipe for disaster.

In dealing with the undoubted hostility and opposition it will meet at home and internationally, such a government must depend primarily on the loyalty and support of the people and especially on those working in the major public and private enterprises in industry, trade and finance, and on the millions working in central and local government. They are the monitoring force, the main source of on-the-spot pressure and initative to deal with attempts at sabotage. This is directly connected with the readiness and ability of capital to hit back, because that depends on what support the capitalist forces can muster amongst, for instance, their managerial and technical staffs, their contacts in central and local government, and amongst politically 'backward' groups (which may include owners of small businesses and some sections of workers). To hit back, capital requires some kind of political base: an important task of a left-wing government and the movement behind it would be to narrow that base to the maximum extent.

Is it inevitable that such a government must face the totally united opposition of all sections of capital, big and small, national and multinational, irrespective of any other affiliations? This may be so, but it partly depends on the strategy and tactics of the movement itself, not only after, but also before, such a government is elected.

We can only speculate on what conditions will exist at such a moment, but the broad strategic lines put forward in this book are not intended as a programme of action in which everything is accomplished in a government's first hundred days or in a single parliamentary session.

Given this limited package of proposals which has wide and well-prepared popular backing, can the opposition be fragmented? We have seen that the AES presents a programme of expansion that can offer growth and profitability for many businesses, large and small. Working-class pressure and bargaining will reduce the rate of return, and monopoly pricing will not be possible, but investment can still take place at lower rates of return; and the role of planning agreements is in part to offer financial support for agreed investment plans. Much depends on whether firms can use their funds in other ways, and the penalties they could face for failure to invest. Such alternative uses of funds for property investment or government bonds would be limited within the UK, and tight exchange controls would make overseas movement of funds difficult for many.

However, as we saw in Chapter 5, multinational companies still have considerable room to counter-attack. But it is also important to remember that the multinationals are *not* homogenous: they come in all shapes and sizes, with assets and activities distributed in different ways between products and countries, and with differing structures and interdependencies within themselves. They also differ politically in their views about their relationships with governments and will, at any one time, take different views of risks and possibilities.

One of the serious threats is, of course, action on an international level, the so-called 'flight from the pound', the outflow of hot money, and the calling in of debts. But there are considerations which other governments, the international financial community, and the multinationals must take into account. Here again, we must remember that a left government will not emerge unanticipated overnight; many adjustments would have taken place long before such an event occurred. I have already dealt with the problem of trade retaliation in Chapter 6 so the arguments need not be repeated. The major contrast with the last financial crisis in 1976, which involved the intervention of the IMF, is North Sea oil which, together with the vast size of the UK import market, can act as a stabilizing force. The possession of oil (needed, for instance, by West Germany) may be a deterrent against creating further instability. In addition, the existence of substantial reserves of foreign currency would be a further line of defence. The world monetary system is fragile and will remain so, since it can only function on the basis of agreement between the major countries (which now include the OPEC states). To destabilize that system for any length of time would create problems for all.

The UK despite its relative decline, remains and will remain a powerful force in the world economy. In that respect it is no Chile.

The left government supported by a democratic movement would appeal for support from the people of other countries, including those who are our major trading and financial partners. We would hope for a response from France, Italy and Spain and even West Germany which went beyond the left; and we would seek support also from other countries who could see the benefits from closer relations with such a government. To the degree that such solidarity develops, hostile action by foreign governments would create unrest within them which, reinforced by the existence of significant economic and political links, would work against such action.

None of this implies that a left government would escape severe pressure and worse, against which it would be expected to act with decision and attack. However, if popular support is sustained, the dynamic involved in trying to carry through a programme vital to the people can – precisely because of fierce resistance from reaction – lead to much more rapid changes than first envisaged. It would be irresponsible for a government of the left to ignore those possibilities or fail to prepare for them; but the degree to which such a period is more or less unstable depends on the specific conditions at the time.

To work towards a Labour government of the left is a major objective. I have tried to answer some of the fears held by many who desire it. The AES, however, is not a programme *waiting* for a government. It is a guide to action. It contains many proposals which are necessary *now* as the economic crisis in Britain deepens; governments can be compelled to respond to powerful pressure. At the heart of the struggle is the situation within the left itself.

The Labour Party, the trade unions and the left

We have assumed so far a movement strong enough to elect a Labour government of the left; but this presupposes a Labour Party which has moved decisively to the left and carried with it large sections of public opinion. Is this likely? Some leftist groups, for instance, believe that the Labour Party must be destroyed and replaced by a revolutionary party.

This book puts the view that the Labour Party cannot be wished away or circumvented. The fact that it has been up to very recent times dominated by the centre and right (and that is still true of the Parliamentary Labour Party) no more makes it a capitalist party than the fact that many unions have right-wing leaders makes them company unions. The Labour Party is the product of the British labour movement and especially of the trade unions. It has established a mass following of many millions, an individual membership of – even at its lowest – hundreds of thousands, and an affiliated membership of more than six million. It is the major electoral opposition to the Tories and the only political force around which an alternative government can be visualized. Its future depends heavily on its relationship with the trade unions who provide almost 6·5 million affiliated members, elect directly 12 of the 26 members of the NEC, and are able to cast their block votes for a further 6. At the 1980 Labour Party Conference the union block votes accounted for around 90% of the total voting power.

The trade unions represent the basic organization of wage and salary earners in all major aspects of the operations of the economy, public or private. They seek to impose a degree of control over the labour process itself. In however sectional a way, they represent the attempt to overcome competition between worker and worker and confront the employers with a single voice. Precisely because trade union organization derives from a common bond experienced by workers it has a powerful and virtually indestructible base *as long as it performs this role*; it necessarily has continuity as compared with ad hoc bodies or campaign groups. Trade unions also have considerable financial strength, however insufficient it may be to do all that is needed.

Trade unions are necessarily in the political arena because all major economic issues concern actions of government or affect them, and because the interests of trade union members cannot be neatly divided into 'industrial' and 'political' ones. The unions involve themselves in wide areas of policy both through their commitment to the Labour Party and also directly as separate unions or through the TUC.

Organizing over 12 million wage and salaried workers, including the majority of state employees and over half the manual workers in the private sector, the trade union movement with its powerful industrial core, together with the Labour Party, constitutes the central force in British politics. What has made the British labour movement almost unique is the fact that the trade unions are so far united around a common centre (the TUC) and are 'geared in' to a single political party, the Labour Party. The future of Britain rests on the way that force is developed and deployed.

The successful fight for the AES and the strategy of which it is part requires a major change in the way the labour and trade union movement functions. This is why we must look at their limitations and weaknesses. A summary account is bound to be oversimplified but can nevertheless provide an 'agenda' for discussion. First: the level of political consciousness within the Labour Party and trade unions is low, and the level of socialist consciousness lower still. Second: the apparatus of the Labour Party and of the unions is to a large degree remote from their membership, and from the millions of their supporters who they do not organize. The Labour Party 'machine' is even further removed from the millions who do not vote Labour, do not bother to vote, or have no vote. Third: the trade unions have grown up in conditions which have created powerful sectional interests within them, which give the media endless material for attack. It is obvious that major changes along the lines of the AES and the election of a left government cannot be brought about unless these weaknesses are overcome. That is the task of the left.

The 'left' is a term much used and rarely defined. For the purposes of my argument I shall define it more narrowly than is usual. I mean by it the body of socialists, however organized, who accept the importance of certain basic ideas, in however 'primitive' a form, such as: ending the dominance of capital, transferring political power to the working people, and extending democratic involvement to the greatest possible degree.

The 1980 Labour Party Conference showed that the left had made a significant advance within the organization of the party; it had a firm majority on the NEC and had sufficient trade union support to create serious pressure for the democratization of the Labour Party. If these measures can be pushed forward, a new phase in the history of that party will be opened up. It is the left which has been the creative force in the party conference and NEC policy formation for more than a decade; its advance is the outcome of the work of all the socialist activists within the movement as a whole, including the Labour Party, the trade unions and the Communist Party. The climate in which it has been able to grow has also been created by many other movements, not least those of the feminists, the anti-racists, the campaign for nuclear disarmament, and all who have taken part in the struggle to advance working-class and popular interests.

I have said the left carries the responsibility for changing the movement, but it is not itself a single cohesive force, and its advance has been violently attacked by the combined forces of Toryism, business, and the right wing within the labour movement. How then is it to advance and overcome its limitations?

The single most important need is for the left to develop a comprehensive strategy.* What sometimes passes for strategy, particularly since the 1980 Labour Party Conference, is that conference decides on a programme for a socialist Britain, this becomes the manifesto of the party on which its election campaign is waged and – if enough seats are won to form a government – that government goes ahead and swiftly legislates for a socialist society. This is not a strategy but a recipe for disillusion.

I would like in a few paragraphs to indicate five important elements of a real strategy.

First: the radical transformation of British society is only possible on the basis of the support of many millions of people organized and unorganized, young and old, men and women, black and white. What is involved now is a campaign and programme for a series of radical reforms of which the AES is a part, based on the needs and concerns of major groups of people. To carry this through the left has to undertake nothing less than the regeneration of the main forces within the Labour Party and the trade unions. In many ways, socialist consciousness in the organized labour movement (like individual membership of the Labour Party) has declined over decades and has to be rebuilt. That regeneration also involves developing political organizations in enterprises, links between Constituency Labour Parties and industry, and also finding ways of increasing cooperation between communists and socialists.

Second: the left must establish the idea that the organized labour and trade union movement should embrace the widest range of concerns. Failure to understand this leaves the field to 'Thatcherism' and will be turned against the labour movement. It must recognize the wide range of class and social forces involved, breaking out beyond the activists, and even the membership, of the unions and the Labour Party. Put

* By far the best available 'model' is *The British Road to Socialism*, Communist Party of Great Britain, 1978.

differently, the movement must be at the heart of a broad democratic alliance. Symptoms of the problem can be seen in the limited attention paid to organizing the unemployed and advancing the rights of black workers. Another vital area is the position of women in the movement, the character of the demands which trade unions make with regard to them, and the movement's attitude to issues which concern the sexual oppression of women. The trade unions have not yet placed the issue of equal pay and sex discrimination high on their agenda for campaigning and action. Trade union committees have relatively few women on them even when they organize large numbers of women. There is little understanding that many current practices and demands which the movement takes for granted, such as the use of productivity agreements or long-service increments, discriminate against women because women are mainly in non-manufacturing employment, and many work part-time and have interrupted service because of motherhood. And this touches only one part of the problem.

Part of the same point is that the left requires to foster and encourage struggles in enterprises and communities which, in the light of the AES, can develop and link with each other to become powerful forces. The working out of local strategies through which people formulate policies for their plant and their community is an urgent task and will enable the AES to become a grass-roots' movement. Projects like the Lucas Aerospace Corporate Plan, which provides detailed proposals for alternative work, are the forerunners of what needs to exist in thousands of enterprises and localities.

Third: the left, within the Labour Party in particular, must rid itself of the narrow view that the Labour Party alone can represent all these movements and interests. Any attempt to *incorporate* all progressive and democratic movements into one party will only hold back the growth of such an alliance of forces; it will also prevent the left from understanding the contribution which these movements make, both in word and deed.

Though it is not this chapter's intention to consider what the left strategy should be on every issue, there is a fourth point which follows directly from our discussion on the survival of a left government. Very few people in Britain understand (or if they understand, disapprove of) the apparatus being constructed to limit and restrict popular activities and struggles. The character of the police force and its functions are being systematically altered and, using the experience of Northern Ireland, the armed forces are rethinking their role with regard to 'civil disorder'. In addition, international tension is being used to foster a climate in which opposition to Toryism can be labelled and suppressed as 'subversive'. The left not only requires to open these matters up to public discussion, which it is beginning to do, but to work out and popularize in much greater detail how the demand for political and economic change, and for greater democracy and extension of civil liberties, can reach the police and armed forces, and be taken up in practical ways – for instance – by local authorities who have certain powers in relation to their police forces.

Fifth: the left desperately needs to encourage and initiate every form of international cooperation, solidarity and exchange between socialist, communist, trade union, and other democratic movements. It needs to support international action on major world issues, in particular for ending military tension and for nuclear disarmament, helping the struggle in the countries of the third world, and joining the battle for human rights everywhere.

The strategic view presented here also has a bearing on the relationship between the trade unions and the Labour Party. It means a recognition by the left that the trade unions are not obstacles to a desirable redirection of the party, but represent powerful forces which must be involved. There will be no overnight victories in this arena. The threat to the unity of the movement arising from serious political differences between the leaderships of important unions, and from the determined efforts by the right wing within the party, makes a *mass* approach even more vital. The left, regrettably, still remains fragmented; working out a comprehensive and realistic strategy will help to knit it together if it is combined with unity in action.

The creation of a broad and popular movement within which socialist ideas grow and spread in many different ways is inevitably a prolonged and complex business. In a way, what must be created is more than is implied by the term 'alliance'; rather the establishment, to borrow the language of the Italian communist Antonio Gramsci, of *political, moral and intellectual leadership.*

Conclusion

By deliberate government action the British people are being made to endure the worst economic and social crisis since 1929. This book has argued that 'Thatcherism' represents a radical and tough strategy which the present leadership of the Tory Party believes will break the bargaining strength of organized labour and lay the basis for renewed capitalist profitability in the longer term. Heavy costs are being inflicted on the majority of the people and on many sections of business, large and small. No recent government has launched such a destructive series of attacks on so broad a front, and struck and hurt so many different groups. The damage, which was already so visible when this book was being written, will become much more severe unless government policies are blocked and defeated.

In this sense the ground undoubtedly exists for a massive movement of opposition which can attach to it even numerous Tory voters and members and undermine the cohesion of the top circle of Tory politicians, financiers and industrialists. Discontent with the *consequences* of Tory policies will intensify, but if that revulsion is to lead to the defeat of 'Thatcherism' (whoever practises it) the labour movement especially must recognize that it is not possible to return to things as they were before May 1979. Tory policy and practice have changed the rules of the game. The recent growth of the left within the Labour Party and some sections of the trade union movement is a signal that this recognition has begun.

Opposition to the consequences of Tory policies does not automatically mean that there will be an overwhelming groundswell to the left. Popular resentment and frustration can after all be channelled in other directions by other parties, such as the Liberal Party; and changes within the leadership of the Tory Party together with modifications of policy cannot be excluded, particularly as the next general election comes into view.

There has to be an alternative which will become all the more attractive as those drawn to it are involved in deciding its character. The AES is intended as a stimulus to fight for changed policies now and to prepare the ground for more far-reaching changes by demonstrating that there is an economic strategy which is viable and coherent.

This book has naturally given great weight to the labour movement, but it is a feature of our time that active independent movements have grown up, such as those of the feminists and amongst ethnic minorities, as well as organized campaigns on major issues such as nuclear disarmament and abortion. In addition, tens of thousands of community organizations have come into being rooted in local needs and conditions. To the degree that these forces can be linked together and contribute towards an evolving common programme, the political and economic scene in Britain will be transformed.

Economic policy cannot be separated from political strategy; nor from morality. The issues at stake include whether Britain is to possess a vigorous productive base or is to be an industrial waste land; whether millions of people are to experience desperate anxiety and rejection or are able to work constructively and live creatively; whether human relationships are to be determined only by the cash nexus (as the logic of capital requires) or by the forces of cooperation. It is a question of *direction*. William Morris, writer, artist, craftsman, socialist, almost ninety years ago set out what is required:

Intelligence enough to conceive, courage enough to will, power enough to compel. If our ideas of a new Society are anything more than a dream, these three qualities must animate the due effective majority of the working-people; and then, I say, the thing will be done.

Appendix*

Effects of the AES on Employment, Living Standards and Growth

The three tables below provide a rough estimate of what effect a programme of economic expansion and redistribution might have on unemployment, wages, welfare services and investment.

Tables I and II suggest what could be achieved in the short run by reflating the economy using existing capacity and without assuming any increase in the long-run rate of growth. Table III sets out some longer-run estimates assuming the economy grows at 3% per annum over a five-year period. Given the assumptions made, we have not provided a detailed account of the calculations, aside from the notes to the tables.

* Prepared by Paul Levine.

TABLE I

Resources and Employment Obtained from Reflating the Economy with some Redistribution

Policy	Resources gained £ million (1980 prices)	Employment effect 000s
Additional resources		
increased use of existing capacity[1]	4,500	330
productivity gains from reducing working week[2]	1,400	460
gains from leaving the EEC[3]	900	–
Redistribution		
reduction in military expenditure[4]	3,300	−110
income redistribution[5]	1,600	–
Total effect	*11,700*	*680*

NOTES

1. Assuming a 10% increase in output in the construction industry and a 5% increase in the rest of industry from fuller use of existing capacity (and that employment would not rise as fast as increased output because some increased output can occur without any increase in jobs).
2. Assuming a 5% reduction in the length of the average working week for the increased labour force, leading to a 5% increase in the numbers employed in industry. We also assume that, because overtime is 40% less productive than normal working, the reduction in the working week will give substantial productivity gains, increasing industrial output by about 2%.
3. These gains arise from ending our net budgetary contribution to the EEC, and no longer requiring to buy foodstuffs from the EEC at prices above the world level. These costs have been added together and government's negotiated repayment deducted.
4. This comes from cutting 1980 military spending by about 30%. We assume a proportionate decrease in the number of service personnel employed. The cut-back in demand for military equipment is assumed to have been more than matched by expansion elsewhere.
5. Assuming (using 1977 estimates) that the share of the top 5% of income units in post-tax income is reduced from 14% to 12%, and that half of that 2% is availiable as new resources (i.e. the top 5% would have saved half of this reduction).

TABLE II

How We Might Use the Increased Resources

Policy	Resources used £ million	Employment effect 000s
Public expenditure		
20% increase in capital spending programme on education, health and housing[1]	700	already included
10% increase in current spending on social services[2]	2,500	350
Investment		
10% increase in fixed investment in private and nationalized industries	2,200	already included
Consumption[3]		
5% increase in total consumption (including 32% for newly employed)	6,300	already included
Total effect	*11,700*	*1 million new jobs*

NOTES

1. Based on 1980 capital programmes and 1979 survey prices, and assuming a 20% rate of inflation between 1979 and 1980.
2. Based on total current expenditure for all central and local government services (excluding law and order) in 1980 and 1979 survey prices, and assuming 20% inflation rate.
3. Newly employed workers would clearly expect to raise their consumption more than the average, which means that the rest would increase by less than the average. We have assumed that the income of the unemployed is 68% of the employed.

Long-term growth

We have used the estimate made by the Cambridge Growth Project that an investment programme 25% greater than in 1979 could raise the growth rate to over 3% during the next decade. That would mean an additional investment of about £5,500 million at 1980 prices. Our reflation proposals could provide about £2,200 million; North Sea oil tax revenues could certainly provide the balance. Our calculations assume that the share of manufacturing stays the same and that consumption, investment and public expenditure all rise by 3% per annum.

TABLE III

Resources and Employment Increase Assuming a 3% Annual Growth Rate over 5 Years

	% growth	Employment effect 000s
Social services	16	560
Leisure[1]		460
industrial workers	5	
entire workforce	2	
Investment[2]		150
initially	25	
additional over 5 years	16	
Consumption[3]		
overall	16	
for newly employed	32	

Total employment effect: 1·2 million approx.

NOTES

1. The working week can be reduced by a further 5% and so create more new jobs. This will mean that the real income of the originally-employed workers will rise by less than it would otherwise. We could for instance have either a 5% decrease in the working week of industrial workers or a 2% decrease for the entire workforce, thus creating 460,000 new jobs.
2. If new technology has a more dramatic effect on productivity than anticipated in the Cambridge Growth Project we could envisage either more output for a given body of workers or the same output with transfer of workers to social services or other sectors.
3. See footnote 3, Table II.

Guide to Further Reading

This guide is not intended to be comprehensive but lists a limited number of works the reader may find particularly useful. Some of the books and pamphlets mentioned themselves contain worthwhile suggestions for further reading.

Books, pamphlets and documents on the AES:

The Alternative Economic Strategy: A Response by the Labour Movement to the Economic Crisis by the London Conference of Socialist Economists' Group (Labour Coordinating Committee, 1980) is a short but valuable and comprehensive review of the AES as a socialist strategy. Written from a more restricted viewpoint but nevertheless very useful is David Blake and Paul Ormerod, *The Economics of Prosperity* (Grant McIntyre, 1980) which contains essays by experts on education, health, transport, etc. A book which played an important part in stimulating the AES is Stuart Holland's *The Socialist Challenge* (Quartet, 1975). Tony Benn's collection *Arguments for Socialism* (Chris Mullin, ed.) (Cape, 1979; Penguin, 1980) is important for its discussion of a number of aspects of the AES, and in relation to the struggle over Labour Party policy and leadership. A leftist critical account of the AES can be found in *The British Economic Disaster* by Andrew Glyn and John Harrison (Pluto, 1980).

For a general account of the development and present state of British capitalism, see *The Political Economy of British Capitalism* by S. Aaronovitch and R. Smith with Jean Gardiner and Roger Moore (McGraw-Hill, 1981).

For overall political strategy see especially *The British Road to Socialism*, CPGB, 1978.

Further relevant material can be found in the 1973 and 1976 Labour Party Conference programmes, the *Annual Economic Review* published by the TUC, and in pamphlets published by individual trade unions such as AUEW/TASS, NUPE, TGWU, CPSA/SCPS and NALGO (obtainable from union offices).

Useful material on community and 'corporate' proposals relevant to the AES can be found in: J. Cowley, A. Kaye, M. Mayo and M. Thompson (eds), *Community or Class Struggle?* (Stage 1, 1977); *Jobs and Community Action*, edited by G. Craig, M. Mayo and N. Sharman (Routledge, 1979); the *Lucas Aerospace Combine Shop Stewards Corporate Plan* (1976); and *Workers' Report on Vickers*, by Hugh Benyon and Hilary Wainwright in association with the Vickers' Shop Steward Combine Committee (Pluto, 1979).

Periodicals

Marxism Today (the theoretical journal of the CPGB) carries a flow of articles on the economy and strategy relevant to the AES. The new *Socialist Economic Review*, vol. 1 (Merlin Press, 1981) also contains much useful material on analysis and policy. Criticism from a leftist position can be found in *International Socialism* (journal of the SWP) and *International* (journal of the IMG). Important articles on the feminist debate on the AES can be found in *Capital and Class*, vol. 11, Summer 1980, *Red Rag* (particularly articles by Bea Campbell and Val Charlton), *Feminist Review* and *Politics and Power*, vol. 1 (articles by Diana Adlam, Fran Bennett, Rosa Heys and Rosalind Coward).

Index

accountability, public, 48, 50, 63–4, 68, 73–4
aerospace, 34, 56, 72, 94–5; public ownership of, 56–7, 61
apprenticeships, 39

balance of payments, 77, 84, 91
Bank of England, 15, 59–60; bank accounts, 59; banks, banking, 6, 20, 38, 58; public control of, 59–61
BBC, 47
Benn, Tony, 11, 64, 109; planning agreements defined by, 63
Beveridge Plan, 98
black workers, advancing the rights of, 122
Blake, David, 32, 39, 80, 98
BNOC (British National Oil Corporation), 14, 54, 71
BP (British Petroleum), 20, 54, 57, 59, 71
British Aerospace, 56–7
British Airways, 20, 57
British capitalism, 21, 109; overseas role and investment, 6, 10–11, 66, 76, 82–3; relative decline, 5–9
British Leyland, 16, 25, 56, 71
British Rail see railways
BSC (British Steel Corporation), 57
building cooperatives and consortiums, 55
building societies, 59
Burmah Oil Company, 54
Butler, R. A. (Rab), 18; Butskellism, 18

Callaghan, James, 5, 14, 30–1, 108
Cambridge Economic Policy Group, 38
Cambridge Economic Policy *Review*, 37
Cambridge Growth Project, 35, 38, 129
Cambridge Journal of Economics, 90–1
campaign for nuclear disarmament, 120
CAP (Common Agricultural Policy), 89, 92, 94; food prices raised through, 24, 91 & n see also EEC
cartels, 59
Catherwood, Sir Fred, 78
CBI (Confederation of British Industries), 18, 26, 69
Chapple, Frank, 108
child benefits, 96, 101; Child Poverty Action Group, 98
Chrysler planning agreement, 16, 64

City of London (financial resources and skills), 6, 58, 76
civil disorders, 11, 122–3
Clegg Comparability Commission, 25
Cole, G. D. H., 68
collective bargaining, 43–4, 72
commerce and trade, 61 see also foreign trade
commodity marketing boards, 94
Common Market see EEC
communications, 34, 61
Communist Party, 2, 45, 68, 73, 109, 120, 121n
compensation (to owners), 60
concensus politics, 17–18, 98, 111
conservation investment programme, 34
Conservative Election Manifesto (1979), 19
Conservative Government: 1970–4, expansion of domestic economy, 7; miners' confrontation, 12, 18; 1979– , 13, 96–100, 123–4; contradictions in policy, 21–7; control of inflation rate, 24–5, 39–41, 77; control of money supply, 22–4, 77; deflation of economy, 19, 21–2, 24, 28, 31; erosion of electoral support, 26–7; exchange controls abolished by, 20, 23, 58, 77, 83; Local Government Bill, 20, 106; monetary policy, 18–19; public spending cuts, 15, 19, 23–4, 96, 102–3; social services policy, 96–100, 102; taxation, 98, 102, 105; trade union policy, 20, 40–1
Conservative Party, 11; election funds, 17n; and election victory (1979), 13–14, 16–18; growing disenchantment with EEC, 89; immigration policy, 19; radical elements, 18
consortiums, 53, 55, 65
construction industry, 26, 32, 62; public control, 53, 55, 61
Co-operative Movement, 45, 62
cooperatives, cooperative societies, 50, 53, 55, 61, 65
cuts see public (government) spending

defence (military) spending see public (government) spending
deflationary policies, 8, 31, 33; Labour, 14–15, 31; Tory, 19, 21–2, 24, 28, 41, 46

74830048